DOLPHINS, MYTHS & TRANSFORMATION

For the dolphins

and whales,

and the people

who feel drawn to them

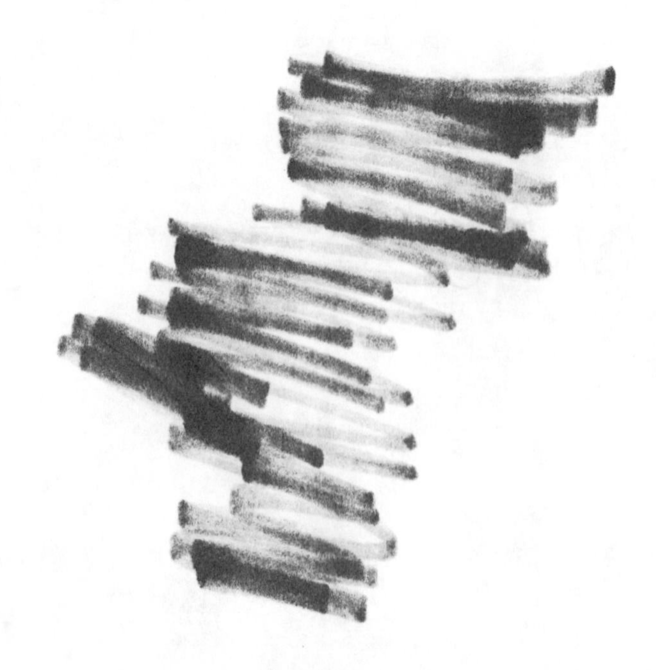

DOLPHINS, MYTHS & TRANSFORMATION

RYAN DEMARES

PH.D.

The Dolphin Institute Press
Boulder, Colorado

ABOUT THE COVER

"Dolphin Serenity" is the creation of the visionary artist John Pitre, who described his inspiration for the image:

> In the equatorial heat of the Pacific Ocean there are places where the shallow coral reefs stretch endlessly and the sea remains glassy calm for a month at a time. Here is where the dolphins live, and so do many of my fond memories.

Printed in the U.S.A.

First printing 2003
ISBN: 0-9720101-0-6
LCCN: 2002091763

LIBRARY OF CONGRESS CATALOGING-IN-PUBLICATION DATA
DeMares, Ryan —
Dolphins, Myths and Transformation /
Ryan DeMares. — 1st ed.
Includes bibliographical references.
1. Dolphins. 2. Human-animal relationships. 3. Animals — Psychological aspects.
4. Animals — Therapeutic use. 5. Human-animal communication.

Front cover illustration:
John Pitre, Pitre Fine Arts, Honolulu, Hawaii.

Author's photograph:
Len Bordeaux, Brant Photographers, Bellevue, Washington.

Cover and text design:
Bruce Taylor Hamilton, Santa Fe, New Mexico.

CONTENTS

PREFACE AND ACKNOWLEDGMENTS

Dolphins, myths, and transformation are three subjects that go together naturally. The connection between dolphins and humans is as old as humanity, and over the millennia has inspired many intriguing myths. In legends, dolphins transform themselves into humans; in life, dolphins often transform the humans who interact with them.

To many people, the word *myth* suggests a half-truth or other fabrication. As I apply the word, myths refer to the constructs through which we perceive and interpret the physical world — constructs that are vital to our culture and lives.

Contemporary Western culture has many myths concerning dolphins. These traditions are not all fanciful tales. Some of them represent modern scientific beliefs, such as the theory that dolphins evolved from a land mammal. Most people of Western culture accept this theory as uncontestable. Yet, evolutionary theory exists alongside ancient native stories and contemporary New Age legends that claim the dolphins came to this planet from another galaxy.

Another modern myth is the cultural belief that only humans possess true language. This myth, as I attempt to show, is closer to being disproved because of recent discoveries that show some species, including the dolphin, *do* have a system of sounds with a complicated structure that fits our definition of true language.

There are many other myths, too, and I present a number of them, including the beliefs concerning the dolphins as healers. We are still discovering the extent of the dolphins' healing capabilities. For many people who encounter dolphins one-on-one, that healing is taking the form of personal transformation. Although the transformation of which I write often involves highly personal experience, transformation has many levels and also implicates our culture and even the dolphins' culture. Among humans, this cultural impact is the result of the dolphins' collective call to humankind. People from many walks of life — psychotherapists and practitioners of the healing professions, artists and other visionaries, environmentalists, and scientists, to name just a few — are hearing the call. Women especially are being drawn to dolphins (in swim encounter groups, the female participants typically outnumber the male participants by about 10 to one). At the same time, increasing numbers of children are discovering a strong connection with dolphins through their dreams, and special needs children are benefiting from time in the water with them.

It is through the dolphins' role as healers that I first heard the dolphins' call in 1996. In addition to finding my own life transformed by the dolphins, I have been observing their effect on others. In *Dolphins, Myths & Transformation,* I share some of my own experiences, including my discoveries about the area of research I pioneered — what it is like to have a peak experience that is triggered by an encounter with a dolphin. Also, at the same time, I have explored many aspects of the human-dolphin connection, including communication projects, animal-facilitated healing, the emerging field of interspecies communication, and the coevolution of two species, each highly evolved in its own right.

This book was made possible through cooperation and inspiration from many others of various species. Foremost, I express appreciation to my colleague and friend Chris Peknic for his abiding love for dolphins and for the vision and effort he has put forth in founding The Dolphin Institute. I also thank him for the encouragement and support he continues to extend to me as I work toward fulfilling my part of our shared vision.

In the course of my inquiries into human-dolphin interactions, I have encountered many people who have been called by the dolphins. Each of them has contributed in some way, directly or indirectly, to my understanding of the human-dolphin connection. Among those who have contributed ideas, experiences, friendship or moral support in the course of sharing their appreciation of the dolphins are Debbie Ault, Lynn Bentley, Sharon Ennis, Lorin Gardiner, Mother Hildegard George, Patricia Weyer, Deena Hoagland, Jody Archer Kennedy, Jeanne Krass, Virginia Lee, Alexis McKenna, Gail Prowse, Scott Olson, and Janice Otero, as well as those who have joined me on dolphin swims and ocean adventures. From each of them, I have continued to learn. My appreciation also goes to Ted Kastelic for his generous spirit and belief in my path.

I also acknowledge Michael Fox and Kevin Krycka, both of whom recognized the value of my academic plans and served as mentors. Others who offered invaluable intellectual and moral support and advice during the course of my doctoral work include Bruce Douglass and Norman Harris, and peers Moses Howard, Dan Page, and Ann Schauber. Penny MacElveen-Hoehn, whom I consider my role model, was a source of wisdom and inspiration. I thank her for emerging in my life at a pivotal time to provide important information that helped me find my path.

Special thanks are due to Hannah-Leigh Bull, Karen Sherman, and Mike Dederer for their careful review of this book while it was at the manuscript stage, and for their many helpful suggestions.

I gratefully acknowledge the generous donation by John Pitre and Pitre Fine Arts of *Dolphin Serenity,* my favorite work of dolphin art, for use on the cover.

Special recognition also is due to the four-legged family that surrounded me thoughout the creation of this book.

Last, but certainly not least, I acknowledge the dolphins and whales themselves for the special dimension they add to my life and the lives of many others.

The social change author Earl Conrad, who, along with his devoted wife of five decades, Alyse, was a dear friend of mine, told me that a book begins to die the day it is published. It is my hope that if books must die, visions and ideals will not. I have drawn upon and, in some cases, expanded upon the presentations of others, including the people and sources mentioned in the copyright acknowledgments section.

Copyright Acknowledgments

AUTHOR'S NOTE: Some names have been changed or omitted to protect privacy. Some narratives have been paraphrased, compressed, or edited for the sake of coherence and grammatical accuracy. The following designations denote trademarked products and registered names: Neurophone for the Neurophone®, a registered invention of Patrick Flanagan. CyberFin for CyberFin™, an invention of the AquaThought Foundation. HeartLink for HeartLink™, a trademark of Brain Actuated Technologies, Inc. Holotropic Breathwork for Holotropic Breathwork™, a trademark held by Stanislav Grof.

DOLPHINS, MYTHS & TRANSFORMATION

THE CALL OF THE DOLPHINS

The first time I saw dolphins in the wild was in 1975. I was running on a beach near San Diego with a friend who was a graduate student studying marine mammals. All of a sudden we spotted fins on the water's surface just beyond the breaking waves. My friend had wanted to swim out to join the dolphins. I successfully discouraged him by saying, "They'll be gone before you get there." I knew nothing in those days about the natural bond that unites people and dolphins or about the powerful, spontaneous dynamics that can emerge when humans and dolphins meet.

Dolphins did not enter my life until 20 years after that near-encounter in Southern California. At the end of 1995, a number of events brought me to a decision that would change my life. After a long career in communications, first as a writer-photographer, later as a journalist, and finally, as a marketing communications consultant, I suddenly decided to begin work on a doctoral degree. I had always possessed an enormous affinity for animals of all species, and the field I chose, interspecies communication, moved my career in communications into that realm. I had no ready-made path to follow, but that was part of the appeal. As far as I knew, no one else had a Ph.D. degree in interspecies communication, and no school offered such a curriculum at any level of study.

But there were some advantages in being the first. I could define the field according to my interests. I soon was guided to an accredited doctoral program that is based on an innovative, multidisciplinary approach, the Union Institute & University. The Union, which is located in Cincinnati, offers a nonresidency program. I would be able to design my own course of study in the field of my choice and complete it where I lived, in Seattle. All of this came together during that pivotal time when the Internet was emerging as a medium of correspondence and networking. The events that followed were unexpected and synchronistic.

While I was preparing my application to graduate school, I spent some time online surfing the Web. Unknowingly, I was about to become part of a network of people whose lives are connected to the dolphins in some significant way — a subculture of which I had previously been unaware. (Now, I often find myself referring to these people as "dolphin people.") On the Web, I came upon a site called "The Dolphin Circle," maintained by Lynn Phillips. My brief correspondence with Lynn precipitated an unexpected series of events when she passed my name along to several other Seattle people who also were interested in dolphins.

One day soon after my e-mail exchange with Lynn, I received a telephone call from a person who introduced himself as Erik Viire. Erik identified himself as a medical doctor and Ph.D. After talking with me about dolphins and interspecies communication for half an hour, Erik mentioned that he was the chairperson of a newly forming scientific committee whose mission was to develop research protocols for investigating the effects of dolphin-assisted therapy. He invited me to become a member of the committee. I had never heard of dolphin-assisted therapy, but I was immediately intrigued by the opportunity.

The committee would be working under the auspices of a nonprofit organization formed by rock singer Toni Childs, who had experienced the magic of a significant interaction with a dolphin. Childs created her nonprofit, the Dream A Dolphin Foundation, to serve as an umbrella organization for dolphin-assisted therapists. She also hoped to bring greater credibility to the field of dolphin-assisted therapy by sponsoring scientific research. I eagerly accepted the opportunity to become involved in the project.

In all, there were four of us on the committee. In addition to Erik and me, there was Lorin Gardiner, a South African woman who was at that time doing a psychiatric residency at a hospital affiliated with the University of Washington, and a Seattle man, Chris Peknic.

From an undergraduate major in marine biology, Chris had gone on to earn a master's degree in social work and develop a clinical therapy practice in New York City. Then, he had felt called to the work of the dolphins. He relocated to Washington state, where he founded a nonprofit organization. He was hoping to foster education about dolphins and to encourage advocacy on their behalf. Chris had named his organization The Dolphin Institute. Now, Erik, Lorin, Chris, and I were bringing together our varied backgrounds and mutual interest in the dolphins to form a team that would aim to make a contribution to knowledge about the effectiveness of dolphin-assisted therapy.

As the months passed and our committee work progressed, we discussed the therapeutic effects that dolphins often seem to have on humans, and the expectations that a funding organization would have regarding research protocols. Part of our groundwork was to identify some of the factors that might influence therapeutic human interactions with dolphins. Might the dolphin's sonar be triggering the effect? Or are the beneficial results that follow time with the dolphins simply the result of spending a vacation in the sun and warm water? No one knew, and determining the answer to such seemingly simple questions would be a complex challenge. Meeting that challenge successfully was vital to developing a baseline for future work.

Amidst these inquiries, one question became foremost in my mind because of my strong interest in the human-animal bond: *If it is the dolphin that is having a beneficial effect, rather than external factors, could another species be just as effective?* I brought this question up to the committee several times during the course of our two years together, but again, no one had an answer. Before long, I began to search for the answer to my question independently of the committee. Eventually, through my reading and by talking with the various people I met who were involved in the field of animal-assisted therapy, I learned that even therapists whose experience involves only domesticated species are likely to regard dolphins as more effective in therapeutic situations. Yet, none of the therapists could offer me any insights as to *why* they thought this, other than to link the perceived effectiveness with the dolphins' advanced consciousness. As I progressed in my studies, I was able to fill in some of the blanks. I learned, for example, that the dolphins' cognitive processes endow the species with a flexibility of behavior that, in some cases, seems to surpass human flexibility. This flexibility is an important part of what makes dolphins different from the domesticated species used in traditional animal-assisted therapy.

The next spring, I traveled to Florida and spent a day interviewing Deena Hoagland, a dolphin-assisted therapist. Not only did I talk with her at length, I also observed her at work with children and dolphins. My connection with Deena had come through the committee. Deena was serving as our unofficial consultant. During my visit with her, Deena recounted her most amazing dolphin experience. The animal involved was not one of those she worked with in captivity. It was a wild dolphin who lives near Jamaica, and the event was, to use her own word, "mind-boggling."

Deena's encounter occurred in 1992 shortly after Hurricane Andrew battered the Florida Keys. The evacuation of the Keys during the storm had created a stressful time for the Hoagland family. After the storm was over, Deena and her husband decided to fly to Jamaica for rest and relaxation. They reserved a tiki hut on the beach at a little lodge.

As they were checking into their hotel, Deena asked whether anyone had ever seen dolphins in the area. The proprietors replied that in the 17 years they had lived there, they had never seen dolphins.

The next morning, Deena looked out the window of the tiki hut and saw a single fin gliding along the surface of the water. It was a dolphin. She jumped into the sea and swam around, listening to the whistles and clicks of the lone dolphin, but never seeing the animal. Each day, the dolphin came back at the same time, and he was venturing progressively closer to her.

Deena's friends and the hotel owners came onto the beach every morning to watch her interact with the dolphin. They were amazed at the dolphin's arrival.

Deena was amazed, too, and not just because the dolphin had appeared, but because he came right to where she was — not down the beach, but right in front of her tiki hut, and he came every day at the same time, "like an appointment."

She invited her friends to get in the water with them, but they declined, saying that the dolphin was there for her. She felt that way, too — that the dolphin had somehow come there just for her, because he knew that she needed to have some fun. The last couple of days, the dolphin allowed her to see him, and on the last day he jumped and whistled and twirled, all at just an arm's length away from her.

Returning home to Seattle after the interview with Deena, I continued to attend the meetings of the scientific committee and support its work. But the day spent with her had led me to rethink my personal focus on the subject. The question of whether Deena had somehow attracted the dolphin to her against the odds was intriguing, but I quickly became more captivated by other possibilities suggested by the experience. I had been reading about the evolution of human consciousness. Peter Russell's book *The Global Brain Awakens* told of a classic experiment that seemed to indicate that humans can affect one another's consciousness, even at a distance. I wondered whether the consciousness of an animal like a dolphin could similarly affect human consciousness. If that is possible, not only would this extend the interactive effects of consciousness into the interspecies dimension, it also could help account for the dolphins' folk reputation as transformers of the people who encounter them.

At the same time, I also was reading the literature of cosmic consciousness, the mystical perception of the entire universe as an integrated and unified whole. Peak experience was mentioned. Peak is a lesser state of transcendent consciousness in which the normal sense of self diminishes or disappears temporarily. An experience that is transcendent or transpersonal occurs beyond the realm of the *persona,* which is our typical state of awareness. When we experience a peak, we are closer to realizing our unity with all of Creation.

In one of my reference texts, the wild animal was listed among the peak triggers. But no studies had ever been made of the wild-animal-triggered peak experience. As I thought about Deena's story, which I had tape-recorded, I realized I already had acquired my first data on the subject. For my formal research study, I would make the first scientific inquiry into the nature of the wild-animal-triggered peak experience, using the dolphin as the model species. Early in my journalistic career, I learned the value of a good anecdote, and the importance of incorporating anecdotal information into my writing for the life and depth it could bring to the overall story. So, as a researcher, I had an appreciation for anecdotal information that a numbers-oriented approach does not support. Instead of doing a numbers-based study, I chose a method that allowed me to look closely at the essences of the experience: the richness of the context in which it occurred, the words the people used to describe their experience with the animal, and the themes that are present. In this way, I was able to analyze the information the people provided without losing the less tangible essences of their experience, the very elements that usually are lost in the process of "number-crunching." My formal procedure also required me to exercise my own imagination at a certain point in the interpretation. For someone like me whose prior career had been based on creative efforts, the research analysis proved to be a wonderful exercise. The end result revealed the essences of the wild-animal-triggered peak experience: a sense of harmony — either the harmony of the pod, harmony with the environment, or a personal sense of harmony; eye contact with the dolphin or whale; the mutual engagement of the human and the animal during the encounter; the dolphin's deliberate involvement; and the feeling of aliveness that resulted for the human.

Most people experience peak at some time in their lives, although they may not recognize the event for what it is. Peak may be perceived in a number of ways. The type of peak that usually occurs in the course of an interaction with a dolphin is the emotional peak, which may also be called the elated peak.

Abraham Maslow, a pioneering researcher in the human potential movement, studied the emotional peak for many years. He defined peak as "the most ecstatic, joyous, happiest, blissful moment in one's life."[1] The moments spent in such a state seem timeless and absorbing. Fears, anxieties, defenses, and inhibitions temporarily disappear as a new dimension of perception emerges. The result is a higher degree of spontaneity and personal integration, and increased expressiveness. Events seem to occur more effortlessly. The realm of positive possibilities suddenly expands.

None of this can be willed, for peaks are invariably spontaneous happenings. However, the stage for a peak can be set, Maslow said, by striving to become composed, stable, and integrated, and by cultivating an attitude of full awareness. When that is accomplished, an external event — perhaps a musical or athletic performance, an experience with Nature, sexual involvement, or, in the case of women, childbirth — becomes the trigger.

Perhaps part of the reason the wild animal trigger is lesser known than most of the other triggers is because we so rarely encounter wild animals and, when we do, it is not necessarily under the best of circumstances.

To be in the presence of dolphins is always a special event, but there is one particular encounter that comes to mind when I am asked about my own peak experiences. One day, while swimming in a bay in Hawaii, I saw the bobbing forms of three swimmers coming toward me through the swells. Thinking I might know someone in the group, I began to swim toward them. As the distance between us closed, I suddenly realized dolphins were accompanying them. By then, I was just yards away from the group, and I could see half a dozen dolphins circling the swimmers. Soon, dolphins began to circle me as well. Sometimes I found myself in the midst of the pod. At other moments, I glimpsed the animals as they darted past.

Suddenly, I was surrounded by at least a dozen dolphins. One singled itself out from the pod and swam straight toward me. Our eyes locked in a gaze. I faced the dolphin squarely and, with as powerful of a kick of my flippers as I could manage without clumsily splashing the surface and perhaps frightening it away, I propelled myself downward through the water. Matching my angle and speed precisely, the dolphin swam alongside me.

Like me, it was rolled slightly sideways, belly toward me, for a full view of its swimming partner. A distance of less than a foot separated us as we moved along together in a perfect harmony of motion. Had I reached out, I could have easily touched its sleek body. In a rush of emotions, I felt an unprecedented joyfulness, a sense of unity with the creature, a feeling of ecstasy. I even had the sudden, irrational thought that I could have died at that very moment, feeling fully satisfied with life. This experience, in itself, seemed enough. Time no longer existed. The dolphin and I seemed to be mirrors of each other.

But my lungs were counting the passing of the seconds, and they began to complain. Reluctantly, I started to arc upward, knowing the dolphin, itself a surface breather, would understand. It did. Staying close to me, it maintained its parallel position just inches from me, never breaking eye contact until I reached the surface. Then it rejoined its kin. Looking down, I saw the entire pod — at least a dozen animals — passing about five feet below me as they departed amidst a cacophony of whistling.

Even then, the experience had not ended. Pausing at the surface to regroup and adjust my fins, I heard a voice say, "We're talking about you." Looking around, I saw the group I had joined. The person who had spoken was smiling joyfully. "We were watching you swim one-on-one with that dolphin. It was beautiful," he explained. Bringing his hands out of the water and moving them along in parallel in an arc, he simulated the undulating duet of movement he had witnessed. As I watched him, the entire experience came back to me vividly in a rush of the same heightened emotions that had accompanied my encounter. My peak had enriched his day, too. We were drawn together into the circle of joy that is created by the transcendent emotions.

In those early days, Chris Peknic and I quickly discovered that we had many similarities in our philosophies and goals. Even before I completed my academic work, we had agreed to team up long-term in facilitating seminars and serving as advocates for the dolphins. The development of The Dolphin Institute became our mutual goal. Then, I didn't foresee taking groups of people swimming with wild dolphins. But eventually, as a result of having personally experienced the powerful presence of the dolphins and loving the ocean as I do, I began to want to share that experience.

Today, when I see the ecstatic faces of people as they emerge from the water, and as they share their stories, I have no doubt that this work is helping to change the world for the better. Many of the people speak of transformation and new-found courage — courage to live their dreams, to overcome fear, to embrace their potential more fully.

There also are other even more compelling reasons for turning our collective attention to the dolphins and whales, urgent bioethical and ecological reasons. Dolphins and whales need our help in reversing or removing the hazards we humans have created — degradation of the natural environment through pollution, toxins, and noise, along with the slaughter of dolphins and whales. Similar threats exist for many species, aquatic and terrestrial. All of the large wild land mammals are in the same kind of peril as the dolphins and whales, and are projected to face extinction within a generation or two, for various reasons. While The Dolphin Institute focuses on dolphins and whales, we also are concerned with living harmoniously with all species. It is our hope that advances gained for dolphins and whales will benefit other species as well.

1

The Transformational Dolphin

One does not meet oneself until one catches the reflection
in an eye other than human.

Loren Eiseley

Many observers of human-dolphin interactions have noticed the dolphins' ability to transform the people who seek them out. Denise Herzing, a biologist who has been studying dolphin populations in the Bahamas since 1985, observed long ago the powerful emotional impact the wild dolphins often have on her project volunteers, even though her research is focused strictly on the natural sciences. She wrote in her boat's log, "The connection people make with the dolphins is worth paying attention to. . . . It's amazing how involved people get in just five days."

Natural sciences training did not prepare Herzing to address the depth of that connection, for even when recast as a research question, the transformational interspecies encounter falls outside the province of the biologist. At times, as her log reveals, she has longed to have a psychologist on board so that an understanding of the connection's dynamics could be achieved. What she did not realize is that even traditional psychology provides little in the way of answers to the questions she was raising. So, the many transformational experiences that occurred aboard her research vessel have remained anecdotes. What has been clear to all, however, is that those who are drawn to the dolphins find a new sense of connection with the Earth, and that the connection helps to bring them into new relationships with the planet and with themselves.

The passage of many seasons in the Bahamas has not diminished the connection that Herzing and her crew see between volunteers and dolphins. In 1997, after I began my research of dolphin-triggered peak experience, her associates were still marveling over the fact that any project volunteer who looks into the eyes of a dolphin "comes away changed, wholly transformed."[1]

In considering why looking into the eyes of a dolphin should be such a universally transformational experience, I am reminded of the mandala, which in art and Jungian psychology is a symbol of wholeness. My own observations and my work with the human-dolphin connection, which draw upon the relatively new field of transpersonal psychology — the psychology of wholeness[2] — have given me the sense that dolphins serve as a living mandala for many people. Dolphins seem to appeal to people who are entering, or are considering entering, unknown or risky territory in their lives back home, and *transformational* is the adjective many people use when describing their experience with dolphins.

Dolphins do seem to be able to touch us deeply, in a way that other species do not. One striking aspect of their influence is that we can feel an emotional response without even being in the physical presence of dolphins. Even a dream interaction with a dolphin may be life-changing if the dream dolphin touches a dimension of us that corresponds to some aspect of our waking reality. That this can happen makes sense when we consider the dynamics of symbols.

Carl Gustav Jung taught that from birth, our human minds are predisposed to perceive in categories called *archetypes*. Some contemporary Jungian psychologists say that a symbolic, archetypal dolphin has emerged from the seas of the collective unconscious. Certain images are known to influence the human psyche profoundly. Increasingly, we are finding that the dolphin symbol emerges in the consciousness of individuals who are undergoing emotional stress. For such people, the symbolic dolphin appears to be an aid in achieving a deeper intuitive understanding of themselves. In the process, they are empowered to cope with the complex demands of life.

The symbolic dolphin can influence people profoundly even when its presence is a mere suggestion. Hillary credits her recovery from cancer to a dream in which dolphins were mentioned but never seen. At the time she had the dream, her health had been compromised for years by a curable form of cancer. Because Hillary had, in her childhood, been traumatized by needles, she preferred to suffer from the disease rather than to accept the chemotherapy treatment that could have cured her. In her dolphin dream, Hillary sensed the existence of incredible love, which infused her with hope and overcame her fears. Interpreting the dream as a sign that she was meant to live, she finally accepted medical treatment and made a complete recovery. Today, she believes that the key to her recovery was the dolphin dream and the sense of incredible love the dream conveyed to her.

As an exemplar of virtuous qualities, there is no more appropriate archetypal animal model than the dolphin. Some people say it is no mere coincidence that dolphins, with their pod consciousness and qualities of joy, playfulness, harmony, are finding their way into our lives and hearts at this particular moment in history. At a time when many people, deprived of any real sense of belonging, suffer from feelings of isolation, insecurity, and powerlessness, these same people say, we may rediscover some of the finer qualities of human nature through our connection with the dolphins.

Jung wrote extensively on symbols as transformers. Since his era, new theories and devices have emerged to help us continue to deepen our understanding of how symbols become catalysts. Author John Van Eenwyk (*Archetypes and Strange Attractors*) described archetypes as "star-gates that give us access to other universes."[3] The archetype should not be underestimated. It can be a powerful portal onto new paradigms and dimensions.

Chaos theory also provides useful models for understanding how symbols serve as catalysts. I can best explain how chaos theory may be applied to illuminate the human-dolphin connection by recounting an experience of my own that does not involve dolphins. One night, during a pause in the rains in Seattle, I was walking my dog along dark streets near my house. As I turned a corner, I heard an unfamiliar and very piercing ringing sound. It seemed to be coming from the end of the street. Following the sound, I came to a vacant house. As I approached the house, I saw a long-haired man pacing back and forth in front of it, in the street. He was not creating the high-pitched noise, but he was adding to it by striking a pair of Tibetan bells. Seeing my glances, he approached me and identified himself as a Microsoft employee who lived nearby. I was hearing the high-pitched ring created by a sump pump that had entered into an unstable oscillation, he said. He was trying to bring the system back into stability through entrainment to an appropriate frequency.

This unlikely encounter was a practical demonstration of chaos theory. Any system that has become unstable is susceptible to being drawn into a new pattern by an outside influence, which is considered the *attractor*. The people who seek out dolphins often seem to be on the edge of change, and the real or symbolic dolphins who emerge in their lives become the catalysts that help to move them into a new psychological state. Eye contact with the dolphin is always mentioned as part of the process, and many people later find they can recreate a similar beneficial state simply by looking at the eye of a dolphin depicted in a photograph.

The wild animal's participation in the peak event is made possible by its lack of fear. Fearlessness of humans is unique to dolphins, which may help account for why a disproportionately high number of wild-animal-triggered peak events involve dolphins. Actually, although the dolphin is frequently pointed out as being the only wild animal that seeks out human companionship, another species, the hedgehog, also is notorious for its lack of fear.[4] I have never encountered any hedgehogs, so I cannot say from personal experience whether a wild hedgehog is inclined to be afraid or unafraid of people. But I have talked with people from the British Isles who can recall seeing hedgehogs in their gardens, and none of them has mentioned having had a peak experience as a result of those encounters. I also have talked with many people who have encountered wild dolphins and whales. (Dolphins and whales are closely related. Both are members of the same biological order, *Cetacea.*[5]) Judging from the tales of those meetings, what consistently occurs when the charismatic dolphin is involved is peak experience. This was fortunate for me, because I had no problem finding people who could provide me with stories for my research project.

The stories that follow provide examples of wild-animal-triggered peak experience, and illustrate the elements and dynamics that are typical of transformational encounters with dolphins. In my experience, only rarely is the wild-animal-triggered peak the result of an encounter with a captive wild animal. The story of Jody and the white (beluga) whale is one of those exceptions.

LOVE EXPONENTIALLY ENHANCED

Jody's experience is a clearly transformational event in which, as is typical of all stories of wild-animal-triggered peak experience, the encounter happened by chance. She had gone to the aquarium to see the otter exhibit, which was housed adjacent to the whale's tank. Not only did she not know in advance that a whale was housed in the adjoining pool, she was completely unaware of the existence of a white whale, a species which lives in subarctic regions.

> A white whale caught my attention. I stopped and looked at it. The whale made eye contact with me. I walked up to the window, and we were eye to eye. Then I had a feeling I've never had before, a feeling of love and connectedness exponentially enhanced. These feelings were powerful. This was a form of communication, a level that the whale and I met on. I thought I could love before that. But I had never experienced anything this powerful. This experience changed the way I perceive what love is, and how I perceive what is possible in terms of connection, and what we can give one another — not only between animals and humans, but also between humans. The experience also changed my ideas about the hierarchy between animals and humans. I felt I was meeting a being who was not just finding a way to meet me in my space but literally allowing me to experience its domain.

Feeling a sense of almost overwhelming love in the presence of dolphins is one of the themes that are frequently mentioned by participants in wild dolphin encounter groups. Lynn, a Santa Fe woman who has swum with dolphins with me, later described seeing three rays of light shining upward through the water during one of our swims. At the same time, she perceived the dolphins swimming nearby to be emitting a loving feeling. Tuning in to that feeling gave her a heightened sense of inner peace and courage. She suddenly felt confident that when she returned home, she would be able to pursue possibilities that she had not had the courage to try before her dolphin encounter week.

Positive emotion arises when a state of harmony is reached, which may help to explain why Jody and Lynn experienced heightened feelings of love in the presence of the whales and dolphins. Some healing arts practitioners have used biofeedback devices such as the HeartLink to identify when the person who is being monitored feels love.[6] Marysol Gonzalez Sterling, a craniosacral therapist who uses captive dolphins in her practice, used the HeartLink during in-water therapy sessions in which dolphins were allowed to watch, swim around, and interact with patients and the therapist.[7] In a dolphin-assisted session held with the parents of two cerebral palsy patients, Sterling and her colleagues tested the monitoring device on the mothers and male therapists. She found that the mothers' love for their children showed most strongly on the HeartLink profile when the parents were in the water in the presence of dolphins and also while they were watching the dolphins through a glass window that opened onto the dolphin pool. Their condition was monitored by measurements that identified which heartbeats were normal and which were abnormal. In the state of love and harmony they attained in the presence of the dolphins, their heartbeats became coherent, an uncommon condition that is identified by comparing normal and abnormal heartbeats.

The HeartLink device also revealed that some of the parents, usually fathers, had difficulty achieving even a small degree of coherence, possibly due to anxiety or worry about their child and also as a result of not being predisposed to feel unconditional love easily. Sterling's observations about gender-related predisposition toward harmony in the presence of dolphins could be useful in establishing a scientific basis for the truism that dolphins tend to prefer women to men.

Of particular interest to me in Sterling's report were her comments about the effect the dolphins' presence seemed to have on her personally. In monitoring her own heart rate, she noticed that as her stay at the dolphin facility progressed, she became increasingly calm and relaxed, yet had more difficulty achieving coherence. She concluded that when the heart is beating slowly, coherence occurs more slowly and does not last as long.

Apparently, in order to achieve coherence, people need a certain level of excitement and involvement in what is happening around them or inside of them. This observation may contain an important clue to understanding why dolphins tend to elicit a sense of love in swimmers, given that most people become excited in the course of a close-up encounter with a dolphin. The following story about Debby's encounter with the orcas illustrates the role excitement plays in an encounter.

RENDEZVOUS WITH THE KILLER WHALES

Debby was on vacation in the San Juan Islands in Washington state when I met her. A mutual acquaintance introduced her to me because he knew she had, years before, experienced a memorable interaction with an orca, the largest of the dolphin family. She felt a special passion for orcas, which she called by their alternate name, *killer whales.* Killer whales are resident in the coastal waters of that part of the Pacific Northwest. As I listened to Debby's story, I was sitting with her on a hillside close to the place where her encounter with the killer whales had actually occurred 10 years earlier. She had been drawn back to the location by her memory of the experience. I was struck with the vividness with which she still recalled the encounter.

> I had always just loved the killer whales, and I wanted to see them. So we took a long trip up the Northwest Coast, not knowing where to go. We ended up on a great little island near the Canadian border. When we arrived, it was almost dark. The day had been dreary and raining. We started driving around the island. Then, just offshore, I saw two fins, and I knew it must be a pair of killer whales although I had never seen a killer whale except on television. I yelled, "Stop the car." My friend said, "No, it's just loons," but I was sure. So we camped near that spot.
>
> The next day, I sat down on the rocks at the water's edge near where I had seen the fins. Sure enough, the killer whales came by again. They swam in really close. I could look down and see the blowhole — an incredible experience. Then one of the killer whales spy-hopped [took a vertical position at the surface for a better view above the water], and I felt he was looking at me. I was perched on a rock that was level with the water, and I knew these resident pods took salmon for feed. I thought, "If that happens to me, it will be an incredible way to go." One huge male looked at me for a long time. His eyes were just above the water line. It all seemed so incredible. I was very excited. I felt like I was meant to be there at that moment.

As aquatic creatures living in an environment that is alien to us, dolphins are, by their very nature, other-worldly. Much of Debby's fascination with the killer whale was related to its *otherness* — the animal's exotic attributes. She had a sense of destiny about her encounter, and had taken little heed for her personal safety. Throughout her trip and especially during those memorable moments on the rocks, her connection with killer whales was what mattered, and she seemingly felt fearless. Her story illustrates the allure of *the other,* as well as the universal human longing to achieve a transcendent experience of oneness with another being.

Although most people today are familiar with dolphins, it was just a few decades ago that Western scientists were encountering them in research laboratories for the first time. An encounter with any dolphin, and especially with the largest of the dolphin family, the orca or killer whale, is an encounter with our oceanic counterpart because it is the top predator in the ocean.

One of the people I interviewed about peak experiences with orcas — which at full adult growth can weigh as much as nine tons — admitted to having thought about what it might be like to join the animal in the water. As an interspecies communicator, I don't mind admitting that I, too, have at times contemplated the possibility of swimming with orcas, especially when I see one in captivity. To want to swim with any of the dolphins and whales seems such a natural desire that I can hardly believe it is not a temptation for all cetacean researchers. So, finding myself in the company of an authority on world orca populations on San Juan Island one day, I could not resist asking whether he had ever entered the water with his research subjects. He laughed and said he had not. Evidently, biologists possess a level of detachment that interspecies communicators do not have.

One scientist has had the audacity to try the experiment with orcas. The site he chose for his adventure was San Juan Island. Trusting in telepathic messages he believes he has received from orca populations indicating that the orcas have entered into a worldwide pod-pact not to kill people, he put a boatload of paying customers in the water in proximity to an orca pod. His objective was to test the therapeutic benefits of the pod's sonar. No lawsuits were brought against him by his customers or their next of kin, so the orcas evidently were not tempted to lunch on the humans milling among them, just as he anticipated. He and his swimmers also had risked legal repercussions, because harassment of wild orcas is among the human activities strongly discouraged by the Marine Mammal Commission. While his actions had no negative effects on the orcas or swimmers, I know from my conversations with researchers based on San Juan Island that his swim-with-orcas experiment did have the effect of outraging the local scientists.

DOLPHIN WITH A MISSION

Jeanne's dolphin encounter occurred on the west coast of Florida at a time when she was at a crossroads in her life. Her life had been centered around her family, but as she and her husband were entering their retirement years, she was beginning to consider other interests and priorities, and intuition was playing a role in her decision-making process.

My husband and I were walking and feeling totally relaxed. Then something told me to look toward the water. I did, and there was a dolphin. I had this most amazing feeling, as though that dolphin had told me to look at him, to make me

> aware that he was there. And then I had an incredible feeling of total exhilaration. It equaled when I had the birth of my children. It was one of those moments that will be with me forever. The dolphin was swimming at the same pace that I was walking. All that time, my heart was racing. I felt so in tune with that dolphin. I felt the dolphin was getting me excited that he was there and making me aware of his presence. He had a message for me — he wanted me to know this was a place that he was safe and I could actually experience seeing him in his natural habitat. He was communicating with me that he knew I was there and also that he knew I was aware of him. The entire experience was totally enjoyable. I had a feeling of almost too much joy.

Jeanne mentioned her racing heart. Strong emotions always involve physiological changes. Abraham Maslow was aware decades ago that the stimulation that comes from peak experience tends to affect the autonomic nervous system and endocrine glands, but the scientific knowledge of his era could not provide him with an understanding of why this should be so. Today, through the work of such biomedical researchers as Candace Pert *(Molecules of Emotion)*, who is renowned for her studies in psycho-neuroimmunology, medical science holds more information about the connection that exists between emotional expression and positive health. These discoveries are significant to the human-dolphin connection because they provide a scientific basis for the healing aspect of dolphin encounters.

Also noteworthy in Jeanne's encounter are her intuitive sense of the animal as a messenger and her feeling that the dolphin wanted something from her. Jeanne intuited a primarily ecological message concerning the animal's existence and its need for safety in the natural habitat. As often happens to those who have had a significant dolphin encounter, an interest in dolphin advocacy work was kindled in her. This is an important element of the peak experience, because in exploring the dolphin as an archetypal figure, we should not lose sight of the broader context in which the species exists. One of the premises of viewing dolphins as archetypes is that animals, like other elements of our external world, tend to mirror aspects of ourself. Yet, as Paul Shepard *(The Others: How Animals Make Us Human)* pointed out, it is arrogant of us to view the animals of the natural world merely as mirrors of a Jungian interior world. "Myths may indeed illuminate unconscious processes, but the context in which that inner world came into being is *ecological*," he said.[8]

The dolphins themselves seem to be reminding us of that ecological context. Dolphin dream symbologist Trisha Lamb Feuerstein has noticed that dream dolphins often seem to serve as environmental messengers. In this way, Feuerstein says, the dolphins seem to be calling us to take heed of the consequences of our actions by observing what those actions are doing to dolphin populations, and will ultimately do to us.

Another striking element in Jeanne's story is the connection she makes between the high of childbirth and the high of her dolphin experience. As a mother, Jeanne has had personal experience that enables her to make a knowledgeable comparison. But I also have found that women who have not given birth to any children intuitively link the emotional exhilaration that occurs as part of these two seemingly dissimilar types of experiences. Some men also sense the connection between dolphins and childbirth. Standing on the deck of an oil tanker in the Persian Gulf, poet Gary Snyder watched dolphins leaping through the ship's bow waves, and recognized metaphors for childbirth. What he saw became poetry: *"dolphins leaping in threes/through blinding inter-/faces . . . ."*[9] His anthologist, Bob Steuding, explained the subliminal connections made by Snyder, created by the dolphins' arching passage through the boat's wave-slip, their "whap" as they hit the water, sounding so much like the slap traditionally administered to a newborn, "the sea as Great Mother, source of all life."[10]

The connection between childbirth and dolphins actually was first made a very long time ago. The Greek root word for dolphin, *delphis* or *delphys,* means *womb.* A few decades ago, all types of dolphins were commonly referred to as *porpoises.* Today, "porpoise" is generally reserved for the smaller dolphins, such as Dall's porpoise, which have certain characteristics that distinguish them from the larger dolphins. I prefer *dolphin* because it recognizes the species' connection to nurturing feminine energy.

Dolphins can empower us to feel love, joy, and playfulness — or so many of the people who swim with them say. Time in the water with dolphins can help us make the shift out of our heads and into our hearts, or give us much-needed courage to meet the demands of life, as it did for Marcella.

Marcella was among the group that joined me in Kailua-Kona, Hawaii, for a dolphin-encounter millennium celebration. As a resident of Manhattan, she later was among those who were close witnesses to the events surrounding Sept. 11, 2001. Marcella was at home when the terrorists attacked the World Trade Center. She watched the crashes on television. Soon afterward, she enrolled as an American Red Cross volunteer at one of the relief centers where many frightened and shattered people, including families of the victims, were flocking for help. For many weeks, Marcella continued to devote long evenings and weekends to volunteering, while continuing to work at her job in the daytime.

At the end of 2001, Marcella told me that her time with the dolphins had given her the personal fortitude to do everything required of her in the aftermath of September 11th. Only when I asked her to share more details of how the dolphins had helped her did I learn that when she was with me in Hawaii in the previous year, she had been recovering from a period of severe clinical depression. From her story, it is evident that she had a powerful experience while she was in the water with the dolphin pod. Through that experience, she gained a newfound sense of courage and strength that eventually empowered her to serve others during an unusually stressful time. She described her experience:

One sleepless night months before I met the dolphins face to face, I wrote,

"Life reminds us that things are to be returned to the earth, and there is a truth underlying even unspeakably difficult losses: As we move through life, we have nothing to hold on to but the experience itself. Our freedom lies in how we choose to deal with loss."

Those words were written just after I was diagnosed as suffering from severe clinical depression. But lack of self-confidence was nothing new for me. All my life, the world has mirrored "the gifted woman" to me, but inside I have always felt like hiding behind the curtains rather than being on center stage. At the time of my depression, though, matters became much worse. I was engulfed by a despair that can be understood only by those who have shared a similar anguish. A black void consumed my feeling of exhilaration and my natural sense of wonder at life's miracles. For six months I searched my soul for some trace of my former wholeness.

Eventually, my search took me to Hawaii. There, at midnight on the last day of 2000, I joined the other members of my dolphin encounter group in tossing floral leis into the ocean in a symbolic gesture. The next morning, we all entered the ocean together and I greeted the dolphins. Despite my initial fears and the weakness of my body, which had been made worn and frail by months of inner turmoil, I could not resist the charm of the dolphins. Watching them swim swiftly and agilely, I realized that I felt a powerful connection with them.

As the pod surrounded me, I opened myself to receive their wisdom. Suddenly, in the vastness of the light that filled the ocean, I was transported beyond time. I lost all awareness of the boundaries of my body as I became connected with the joy that fills the universe — a feeling that I had known earlier in my life but had been out of touch with for a long time. On that day, in the ocean, my heart was filled with overwhelming joy as something extraordinary, a transformational force, touched me.

Later, back home, I was able to continue to tap into that same deep well of compassion, infinite calm, and fearlessness. I gained the abiding sense that I had blossomed as a person. I feel now that this experience prepared me for what was to come nine months later.

Because of the time I have spent in various parts of the world, the sight of blood and death was already familiar to me. My career has taken me to places where bombs part human limbs from bodies, and children do not know the meaning of the word *peace*. But nothing about my life could have prepared me for facing the tragedy that occurred in New York. Until then, childlike, I had believed that angels could fly; on September 11th I saw them dive into the concrete. The blue sky over Manhattan became so ominous even the birds vacated it.

On that first day I wandered the streets aimlessly for hours. People whom I had for years greeted on the way to work in the morning had suddenly disappeared — either missing or dead. In a city known for toughness and detachment, even men were weeping in the streets. Returning home finally, I sank to the floor of my apartment. Then, in an instant, I realized it was time for me to move to center stage. Blood donations were needed. The city was recruiting volunteers. I walked to the Family Assistance Center and signed up for a volunteer post that I occupied for the next three months.

Each evening as I came to the center I had to walk along a wall plastered with pictures of the deceased. We volunteers called this corridor the "Bear Walk" because it became lined with stuffed teddy bears sent by the people of Oklahoma City to families which had lost loved ones.

As the weeks passed, I witnessed the anguish of the survivors, the families, and the displaced people as I translated for them and escorted them through the facility to get financial help from the different agencies. They told me their stories in excruciating detail.

What came to matter most about my life in those days was the ocean of peace and courage that I could call up from memory. Surrounded by people who had been forced to stop and take stock of their lives, I rejuvenated my spirit by remembering what it was like to look into the eyes of a dolphin.

I have related a variety of experiences, but certain themes are common to all of them. In each case, eye contact was made, or there was another indication that the animal was intentionally involved in the interaction. Positive emotions and responses were aroused. These themes are typical of the dolphin-triggered peak experience. Similar themes can be found in the popular literature of human-animal interactions, such as in a story told by veterinarian-author Allen Schoen about his encounter with sea lions in the Galapagos Islands. During that experience, which he recounted in his book *Love, Miracles, and Animal Healing,* Schoen was accepted into the sea lion colony and participated in the rookery's quiet sunning routine on the rocks and, eventually, their joyful cavorting in the water. From his description of the elements of eye contact, the animals' intentional welcoming and acceptance of him, and the harmony, joy, and sense of connection that pervaded the encounter, parallels with the dolphin-triggered peak are evident.

Some people believe they are not capable of experiencing peaks. In speaking of this problem, Abraham Maslow called such people *nonpeakers.* It is not so much that they don't have peak experiences, Maslow said, but rather that they are afraid of owning their peaks. In their fear, they may suppress the experience, or deny it, or turn away from it, or "forget" it.

As he investigated the history of various nonpeakers, Maslow found that their way of life forces them toward materialism, mechanism, or extreme rationalism — all mindsets that often regard transcendent experience as a level of insanity, an undesirable irrationality, or a loss of control. Additional explanations for not being capable of "highs" include being means-oriented and not seeing sufficient practical outcome in the experience, or being so other-directed as to be out of touch with oneself. Yet, I have witnessed what can happen when a nonpeaker meets dolphins. The results may be remarkable. One incident that stands out occurred during a trip to Hawaii. I had spent a morning in the company of half a dozen other people, paddling around a bay in kayaks. After a couple of hours, we all lifted our paddles out of the water and drifted, close together. Suddenly, a pod of dolphins emerged all around us — on every side, close enough for us to reach out and touch, although we didn't try. We just continued to sit quietly in our kayaks. None of us tried to slip into the water alongside them. None of us even moved or spoke. Then, something very peculiar happened. As the dolphins drifted placidly at the surface just a foot or two away, a sense of expansion seemed to stir within my heart and solar plexus. My journal entry says, *As we sat encircled by the dolphins, some of them made spins. I felt a stirring in my chest, an odd feeling I don't recall ever having experienced before. It felt like an expansion or a rising. It didn't last very long, mainly, I think, because Chris* [Chris Peknic, the group's leader] *was saying we had to go.*

I did not mention the unfamiliar, exhilarating sensation I felt to anyone else. So I was fascinated to learn a few days later that another member of our group, a quiet, middle-aged man who took no particular interest in dolphins, had an experience very similar to mine and, apparently, at the same time. "When we were drifting in the middle of the pod," he recalled, "I felt something happening within myself that I cannot find words to describe. But I will remember it for the rest of my life." This incident serves as an example of how deeply the dolphins can affect even someone who is normally controlled and unemotional.

For many people, dolphins, like the mandalas of Jungian psychology and Eastern tradition, seem to facilitate an experience of wholeness, and they do it in a way no other animal species comes close to equaling. Trisha Lamb Feuerstein, who has for many years been researching the psychological and cultural significance of cetaceans, says dream dolphins and whales seem to be calling upon us to transcend our fears by moving out of our minds and into our feelings. The process reconnects us with peace, joy, bliss, and serenity. The same seems to be true of the physical dolphin. Whatever the reason for the dolphins' extraordinary influence, we humans are uniquely and profoundly influenced by the dolphin presence and archetype.

2

The Language Puzzle

Sometimes I dream I'm swimming along, alone, when I hear
dolphins near me, and I understand what they're saying
to each other. I can understand their language.
It's farfetched, I know . . .
What can I say? That's my dream.

Kathleen Dudzinski

Give orange me give eat orange me eat orange give me eat
orange give me you.

The signing chimpanzee Nim Chimsky

In the creation stories of Western science, the primordial ancestors of the dolphins and whales are amphibian. In time, these partially aquatic, partially terrestrial creatures chose land over sea, and evolved into the group of mammals known to zoologists as the furry, four-footed creodonts. Scientific texts describe the cetaceans' land-based ancestors as being reminiscent of either canines or bovines.

In dogs, the position of the ears, whether forward or back; the hair, flat or erect on the back of the neck; the turn of the eyes; the lip's curl, or its contraction to show fangs; the tail wagging, or, perhaps, the tail curled between the legs, all give clues to the animal's inner state. But after the creodont returned to the sea and began the next phase in its evolutionary journey, most of those external cues were lost. In their place, the prototypic dolphin evolved whistling capabilities. Some body language remains, of course, but it is largely through sound that dolphins express themselves. Their high-pitched clicks and whistles are produced by the release of constricted air through the nasal passages, finally exiting through the blowhole on the top of the heads.

Most cetaceans possess two kinds of voices. One consists of whistles and is used for social communication. The other consists of clicks and ultra-high sonics, and aids the animal in navigation and location of submerged objects. These two voices can be projected simultaneously. The whistle is characteristic of the species, but it also is individualized, giving each animal a unique sound called its *signature whistle.* Dolphins are born with their signature whistles already developed. The signature whistle ensures that each member of the dolphin community can recognize other dolphins when communicating within the pod. One of the mysteries of dolphin communication is whether the dolphins' whistles are components of a true language.

The question of true language also is one of the broader puzzles of the animal kingdom. In the 18th century, zoologist Thomas Huxley proclaimed that man alone possesses "the marvelous endowment of intelligible and rational speech [and] stands raised upon it as on a mountain top."[1] In the tradition of Huxley, Western science views signal-based nonhuman-animal language as inferior to human language. Human language alone is considered true language, because it possesses semantics (grammar) and syntax (word order). Despite the fact that as much as 75 percent of the meaning in a face-to-face human conversation may be communicated through body language and intonation, the presence of a structured sentence serves as our ultimate test for language.

Yet, the prospect of interspecies communication by any standard so intrigues humans that researchers have gone in a variety of directions to explore the possibilities of nonhuman language capabilities. Dolphins and primates are the focal point of the most prominent of the language research projects, and each of these long-term programs has made valuable knowledge contributions to the study of animal language.

The primatology studies have shown that, other than humans, the species that belong to the great ape lineage are not capable structurally of articulating words. Meanwhile, analysis of dolphin signals has revealed the "building blocks" of speech. Orcas are known to communicate in dialects that are distinctive to the various pods, and to possess a vocabulary of at least 15 phonemes (units of speech). Because the orca has one of the larger brains on the planet, it would not be too surprising if a researcher demonstrates beyond any reasonable doubt that dolphins possess true language. But, surprisingly, prairie dogs may also have a similar gift.

In Northern New Mexico, which currently is my home, one of the local controversies concerns the fate of prairie dogs who are being displaced by land development. Many people here respect prairie dogs as an important part of the native ecosystem, but a minority consider them to be disease-ridden vermin deserving of extermination. Even among their advocates, few realize that prairie dogs may, like dolphins, hold the key to discovering true language in the nonhuman animal kingdom.

A biologist who has been researching prairie dog populations for three decades is coming forward with proof that these rodents possess true language — a startling discovery in view of the species' comparatively rudimentary brain. The researcher, Con Slobodchikoff, is a professor of biology at Northern Arizona University.

In *Kinship With the Animals,* Slobodchikoff described how he, students, and colleagues have spent years trying to decode prairie dog language and determine what prairie dogs are able to communicate to one another. His studies have shown that much more awaits discovery.

To date, nine words (units of speech that are used nonrandomly) have been identified by his research. Some of these words always occur at the beginning of a chatter, some are always in the middle, and others are always at the end. Slobodchikoff would like to find a Rosetta stone to decode prairie dog language. In the absence of such an aid, he and his fellow researchers are studying the behavioral contexts in which these chatters occur, in the hope of discerning additional meaning. The scientific community is reluctant to take seriously the possibilities raised by the prairie dog research, and Slobodchikoff is not able to get all of his findings published.

Curious about what the prairie dogs talk about and how they do it, I drove to Flagstaff to meet Slobodchikoff. He described to me how, working with sonograms (voice prints) recorded in the field, he has made a number of discoveries, including the observation that prairie dogs can convey abstract concepts to other prairie dogs. Their chirping speech, which sounds almost birdlike, incorporates descriptive information about colors, size, and shape. He told me,

---

> We do not have a Rosetta Stone for the social chatters. However, we do have a Rosetta Stone for the alarm calls which the animals produce when a predator appears. We can record the calls and the prairie dogs' escape behaviors, and we can play back the calls when the predator is not present. Because we know who the predator is, we can decipher those alarm calls. We have found that there are different words for different predators. In our published work, we have identified calls for coyote, domestic dog, human, and red-tailed hawk. We are now submitting a paper showing that there are other calls for badger, fox, antelope, and domestic cat.
>
> When we analyze the structure of the calls, we find that not only can prairie dogs identify the species of predator, they also can describe some of the physical features of the individual predator — the general size, shape and color of clothes of a human, and the size, shape, and coat color of a coyote or a dog. When the prairie dogs see an object that they are totally unfamiliar with, such as a silhouette of an oval, all the prairie dogs in the community consistently describe the oval in the same way. This suggests a sophisticated form of communication that can provide information about both predators and non-predators in the general environment.

The only other nonhuman terrestrial species known to have such a sophisticated system of communication is the vervet monkey.

"If prairie dogs do have true language, that raises the possibility that other species with rudimentary brains also might have true language — possibly even cats and dogs," I ventured. Slobodchikoff nodded in agreement. (I do not actually believe that domesticated dogs and cats are likely candidates for true language. My sense is that even if those species innately possess the capability, those who share their lives with us have been too influenced by human culture. Feral cats, however, may offer a window of opportunity for language research, or so it seemed to me after informally observing the vocalizations of a feral I detained in my house for six months.)

An even more obvious possibility is true language in the context of a comparatively sophisticated brain. The dolphin brain has a well-developed structure, the neocortex, that is larger than the human neocortex. Yet, despite these promising features and decades of language research, the archives of animal language research contain little information about dolphins and true language. If language research is being conducted with prairie dogs, why is similar research not being done with dolphins?

As it turns out, the U.S. government apparently is exploring the natural language capabilities of dolphins, but is keeping its methods and findings secret. Still, word has leaked out to the public. One of the pioneers of animal-assisted therapy, Mother Hildegard George, was a resident of the Hawaiian Islands during the late 1960s. She remembers the Navy's communication experiments with dolphins during that era. The news got around among the local population that the military was training dolphins to assist in submarine rescues. She says that the dolphins were carrying messages to the surface, and that the level of communication occurring between humans and dolphins "was just incredible." What she was describing can only be spin-off from one of the lesser-known chapters in the history of dolphin language experiments, a story that began in the 1960s and involved a mathematician named Dwight Wayne Batteau.

Batteau was the senior scientist on a government project to develop a common language between human and dolphin. The Navy was interested in determining the feasibility of producing human-to-dolphin and dolphin-to-human translators, electronic devices that enabled interspecies communication through a system of whistling exchanges. Project funding came through the U.S. Naval Ordnance Test Station in China Lake, Calif., where the project was initiated. The research was soon moved to a lagoon on a small island near Oahu. Its final phase began in December 1966 and the project became classified the next year.

The goal of Batteau's research, which was called the Human/Dolphin Communication Project, was to communicate with the dolphins in their natural whistling language. For this purpose, Batteau designed an underwater sound box, technically known as a *transphonometer,* that could turn the human voice into a variety of low-pitched and high-pitched whistles. Essentially, the instrument converted human language into whistles by shifting frequencies in a way that made the human voice higher. In this way, human vocal sounds, which normally are at the extreme lower end of dolphins' sound bandwidth, were shifted up into the dolphins' naturally high range. By using the transphonometer in combination with a Neurophone, the project team was able to hear the full range of dolphin sounds, which extend well beyond the normal limit of human hearing.

Batteau built a structure into the whistles produced by the transphonometer so he could give various commands to the project's dolphins. The Hawaiian language, which is rich in vowels and has only 14 phonemes, was more suitable than English for the work. Batteau's dolphins responded well to commands made in the artificial whistling language. The researchers also tested whether the dolphins could learn different responses to correspond to word order variations. In the course of the experiment, the dolphins mastered more than 30 Hawaiian words.

The project team included two other ingenious inventors, Kenneth LeVasseur and Patrick Flanagan. Both LeVasseur and Flanagan have in recent years made new information public regarding their experiences on the Human/Dolphin Communication Project. In 1996, Flanagan reconfirmed publicly some of the features of the translator and the fact that the researchers had, through the use of the device, been able to perceive more of the intricacies of the dolphin language.

"The translator was able to decode human speech so that complex dolphin whistles were generated. When dolphins whistled, the translator would produce human speech," Flanagan said.[2] The project team also used the device in reverse, to encode dolphin whistles into human speech. In this manner, the project team achieved communication with two captive dolphins.

In terms of honoring dolphins' own native intelligence and natural communication modes, Batteau's line of inquiry seems clearly more appropriate than anything attempted since his time.

The Human/Dolphin Communication Project ended under tragic circumstances. Shortly before the conclusion of its initial phase, Batteau drowned while swimming in the ocean, the apparent victim of a heart attack. In a final report to the Navy, his colleagues stated that the project had established a basis for the development of a language between human and dolphin.

Yet, despite the promising results, scientists brought in by the Navy to review the research team's work discredited Batteau's conclusions. They portrayed the research results as undermining the project's original hypothesis that dolphins have the degree of linguistic comprehension and flexibility necessary for language capability. It was not until years later, when disinterested parties revisited the project's final report, that the truth reemerged. Batteau's dolphins had, indeed, demonstrated an ability to learn, memorize, and emit whistles. Teaching them a whistled language, which logically would be far better suited to their natural characteristics, not only made sense in theory, the Human/Dolphin Communication

Project had shown the approach to be workable. Reexamination of Batteau's work suggested that the Navy may have deliberately withheld the project's most important findings.

The final report for the Human/Dolphin Communication Project can still be obtained today under the Freedom of Information Act, although it has been heavily censored. Hardware diagrams and specifications are said to be missing. However, at least one copy of an uncensored version of the report is in general circulation. Those who have seen it confirm that Batteau's conclusions point to dolphins as possessing a whistle-based language.

As soon as the results of the experiment were clear, the government put a secrecy order on the neurophone used by the Human/Dolphin Communication Project. The transphonometer vanished entirely.

In the late 1990s, Ken LeVasseur stated on his Web site that the Navy is still using frequency-shifting translators to communicate with dolphins, and that their devices are based on the Human/Dolphin Communication Project's work.

While Batteau was conducting whistle-based experiments in the mid-Pacific Ocean, John Lilly was carrying out his own landmark investigations into dolphin language capabilities, at a research station he established in the mid-Atlantic Ocean, in the Virgin Islands.

Lilly had made his initial contact with dolphins at Marine Studios in St. Augustine, Fla., in 1955. At that time, he was the quintessential researcher, maintaining detached objectivity as he planted electrodes in his subjects' gray matter. Later, he watched them expire as he injected fluids into their brains in order to obtain fresh cell specimens. Using such techniques, he and his colleagues made the scientific community's first inquiries into dolphin neuroanatomy and physiology, and discovered the species' voluntary breathing system inadvertently when an anesthetized dolphin suffocated.

Eventually, Lilly grew more subjective and, at the same time, more interested in communication, which he defined broadly as the exchange of information between two or more minds. He quit his work with the National Institute of Health and drew upon his family wealth to found the Communication Research Institute on St. Thomas Island in the Virgin Islands. His intention was to focus on language experiments, and his approach initially consisted of encouraging dolphins to mimic English. (The dolphin's blowhole mechanism and its natural aptitude for mimicry enable the animal to do some amazing things with sound, including a fair approximation of human language.) Lilly's language research ended abruptly in 1966, when several of his captives died simultaneously (a suicide pact, he said). From that time on, he considered it unethical to keep captive dolphins.

While Lilly's dolphin-language experiments were in progress, language experiments with the great apes were proceeding down an entirely different track. Researchers had determined early on in primate studies that although chimpanzees can learn to understand human-produced sounds, they lack the vocal apparatus necessary to reproduce human language. What the chimpanzee does possess is a natural language based on gestures, which makes it possible for us to communicate with chimps by teaching them American Sign Language.

Roger Fouts is one in the line of researchers who have explored primate communication. Though nothing as dramatic as a language translator has emerged from primate studies, some important new insights into human language production have been achieved as the result of Fouts' work with the chimps. These insights include the theory that the evolution of the human brain was shaped by movements of the tongue.

Fouts' conclusions came as the result of decades of working with gestural language. However, not unlike Lilly's own evolving priorities, Fouts has, in recent years, become less research-oriented and more concerned with allowing his primate family to live as normally as possible in its social unit on the campus of Central Washington University in Ellensburg.

Other long-term communication projects involving the great apes also have made considerable progress. Susan Savage-Rumbaugh maintains a research facility in Atlanta, Ga., where she works with bonobos, another member of the great ape family that is closely related to chimpanzees. She has taught the bonobos to communicate their needs to humans by using lexigrams, symbols on switches that are arranged in an array for easy manipulation by the bonobos' fingers. When a switch has been triggered, the lighting increases so that it stands out against the lexigram array. Read in sequence, lexigrams can form a sentence.

Lexigrams actually had been tried with the great apes even earlier, during John Lilly's days as a language researcher. Lilly knew about that approach but had not found it suitable for dolphins. He pointed out that dolphins and humans share a sophisticated capability for using sound for communicative purposes, a capability not shared to such an advanced extent by the apes, who are limited to signal-based language. It made no sense to him to have dolphins push switches with their jaws when they were naturals at controlling sonic output with great sophistication. Instead, he chose to focus on the species' natural capability for producing and understanding complex sequences of sound.

At the same time, incidents were occurring that alerted Lilly to the possibility of previously unsuspected dimensions in dolphin communication. One of these involved an exchange that he interpreted as demonstrating a dialogue. A male and female dolphin pair was separated in the pool by a sheet metal panel. As Lilly listened to their whistles, it seemed clear to him that the two dolphins recognized each other's sounds through the barrier. They tried to leap high enough to glimpse each other. Failing in that, they fell silent for a while. Finally, the male launched into what seemed to be an extensive monologue. When the female finally responded, the male kept silent until she was finished "speaking." The exchange continued in this alternating manner, convincing Lilly that a conversation was in progress.

Lilly eventually launched a computer-based communications project, JANUS (Joint Analog Numerical Understanding System), with the hope of interconnecting sonic and visual signals. However, while his earlier dolphin experiments were in progress, Lilly had become engrossed in personal experimentation with mind-altering drugs. He acquired the reputation of being a maverick scientist, which estranged him from the scientific community. His loss of credibility ended his mainstream career, but his early efforts in teaching English to dolphins earned him a place in the minds of many people as the pioneer of interspecies communication. To the end of his days (in 2001, at age 86), he enjoyed a substantial cult-like following.

In Hawaii, after the close of Batteau's Human/Dolphin Communication Project, the Navy began to funnel its human-dolphin communication research money to Louis Herman, who is an experimental psychologist. In Herman's studies, which continue today, whistles are not being used as information carriers, and dolphins are not being encouraged to produce language. Neither are the dolphins encouraged to use acoustics to communicate back to their experimenters. Instead, his team has experimented with an elaborate command communication system that tests the extent of dolphins' capabilities for responding appropriately to commands involving labeled objects.

I have not been able to tour Herman's laboratory, as I had hoped to do one day. I contacted his organization (ironically, it is called the Dolphin Institute, like my own) and requested permission to spend part of a day observing his project team's research activities. I was turned down, with no reason given. However, I have learned from students who have had access to Herman's facilities that new methodologies are being incorporated into his experiments, inspired by the bonobo research. Despite Lilly's earlier rejection of them, lexigrams evidently have arrived on the dolphin language research scene.

Meanwhile, Kathleen Dudzinski has emerged as the promising new researcher on the dolphin scene, reflecting current trends in animal experiments — the migration out of the laboratory and into the animal's territory. A relatively recent Ph.D. with a focus that combines behavior and communication, she achieved her current prominence in 1998 as the result of being tapped to become the human star of the IMAX production *Dolphins*. As a mainstream researcher, Dudzinski operates under the assumptions that dolphins lack both a specific dictionary of signals and a vocabulary of "words." Unlike the earlier generation of animal language researchers, who work with captive animals, her approach is to go into the pods' ocean habitat and study the common signals made between dolphins according to context, in order to connect routine behaviors to meanings.

Today, largely due to Lilly and despite scientific denial of the existence of true language in dolphins, popular wisdom continues to perpetuate the belief that dolphins possess a high-order language. Periodically, syndicated newspaper articles appear that provide information debunking this particular belief. One example is a *New York Times'* article that quoted an unnamed biologist as saying that dolphins do not have a real language apart from the unique whistles some species use to identify themselves. However, the *Times'* report did acknowledge that the dolphins' whistling is an indication that dolphins have individual identities, an attribute the reporter acknowledged is unusual in animals other than humans.

An acquaintance of mine, Joy, told me a story about a verbal communication she received from a captive beluga whale. She had been standing poolside for awhile, and the beluga had seemingly been trying to teach her something. The animal must have decided its human subject was a disappointingly slow learner, for it became increasingly frustrated in its attempt to communicate, or so Joy intuited. Finally, it was time for her to leave. As she turned to go, she heard the beluga call after her: "Good-bye!" Joy, who takes her interspecies ambassadorship very seriously, was brought to tears by the experience of suddenly being addressed in English by a whale.

I asked Joy whether she had checked with the aquarium staff to see if the whale had ever been involved in language lessons. She had not. The whale's farewell may have produced an emotionally charged moment for Joy, but it created a puzzling mystery for me. Some months later, though, I came across an interesting bit of information that seemed to help explain the incident. Although dolphins have for practical reasons been the species of choice for language experiments since the days of Lilly, beluga whales actually are better vocalization mimics.

More important, though, is the fundamental yearning revealed by Joy's reaction to the beluga. It is this aspect of human nature that I am most drawn to consider when I reflect upon interspecies communication research. The yearnings of the human psyche do not reveal themselves through the work of experimental scientists; their exploration falls, rather, within the domain of humanists and poets. The scientist-poet Loren Eiseley addressed these matters in his essay "The Long Loneliness." He wrote, "When we were children we wanted to talk to animals and struggled to understand why this was impossible. Slowly we gave up the attempt as we grew into the solitary world of human adulthood."[3]

Eiseley was at the zenith of his literary career in the days of Lilly's language inquiries, and the work of the animal communicators did not escape his attention. "The dolphins show a degree of initiative in experimental communicative activity unmatched by man's closest relatives, the great apes," he observed in an essay that concluded on a characteristically poignant note:

> It is worth at least a wistful thought that someday the porpoise may talk to us and we to him. It would break, perhaps, the long loneliness that has made man a frequent terror and abomination even to himself.[4]

Today, we are struggling with a new set of terrors, and our tools for ending humankind's continuing isolation include cell phones and e-mail. But dolphins are still a part of our culture, whether as physical animals or as archetypes and symbols. Their reassuring presence holds a prospect not available a generation ago, of not just a creature with whom we might one day talk, but of a being that is capable of affecting us deeply, as part of a transformational alliance with a different kind of consciousness.

3

Some Dolphin Basics

The dolphin hears in a way that resembles the way a roentgenologist uses x-rays to see.

Karl-Erik Fichtelius and Sverre Sjölander

John Lilly's early language experiments involved subadult Atlantic bottlenose dolphins who were about six years old because at that age the brain of that particular dolphin family is roughly equivalent in size to the adult human brain. At maturity, the Atlantic bottlenose dolphin has a brain weight of about five pounds, which is about 40 percent larger than the average 3-pound human brain.

If you look at the comparative brain features of human and dolphin brain specimens (and there are places the public can do so, such as the Vancouver Aquarium in British Columbia), you will notice immediately that human and dolphin brains are strikingly similar. When Lilly, who was trained in neuroscience, looked at the dolphin's large brain, he wondered whether the dolphin's mind might also be larger than our own. He began to suspect that the dolphin has the capacity to engage in a complex, higher, more complete kind of communication than we humans possess.

Most scientists are more conservative. Their usual speculation is that the vast so-called silent areas of the dolphin brain that remain a mystery to science are actually used in the processing of acoustic information, a reasonable supposition to apply to an animal that navigates by biosonar. Mere brain size is not considered an indicator of a superior intelligence, because it may be a reflection of having to support and maintain a greater body mass. Scientists prefer to apply a measure called *encephalization quotient,* abbreviated EQ, in assigning a hierarchy of comparative intelligence. This scheme places our own species in top ranking. Our human EQ is higher than the dolphins' EQ by a comfortable margin. But the dolphins' EQ compares favorably with the EQ of our nearest animal kin, the chimpanzees, whose EQ is less than half of dolphins' EQ.

The Nobel laureate Francis Crick has speculated that brain size in mammals is related both to metabolic rate and to whether or not the particular species experiences the rapid eye movement stage of sleep, which indicates dreaming. Crick has observed that dream sleep is absent or reduced in the nonhuman species that have particularly large brains. Brainwave analysis shows dolphins to have patterns which in humans correspond to sleep or deep unconsciousness (delta), to meditation or mystical states (theta), and to states conducive to accelerated learning, self-programming, and self-healing (alpha). But dolphins do not seem to dream, and, in fact, they sleep only one-half brain at a time. They are conscious breathers, and part of a dolphin's brain has to be awake in order for the animal to continue breathing.

In humans, the neocortex is involved in creating, innovating, and reasoning. In dolphins, the corresponding structure is much thinner than in the human neocortex, but it covers 98 percent of the animal's cortex, which is more area than it covers in the human brain. Also, it is more enfolded, giving the dolphin brain more surface area than the human brain. Just as in humans, the dolphin brain has rich interconnections between the right and left hemispheres. In fact, there are more interconnections between the dolphins' two hemispheres, suggesting the possibility of a more holistic use of their brains.

In the folk wisdom that has arisen around dolphins, dolphins are held to equal or, perhaps, even to exceed humans in intelligence. Their superiority is clear in certain regards such as navigation. Thirteen kinds of dolphins and whales range the vast expanse of the ocean using navigational skills we do not yet understand, and navigational capability is a form of intelligence. The evolution of a high degree of empathy and synchrony may be another of the dolphins' significant species achievements. Years in the field among wild orcas have convinced Alexandra Morton that those two attributes — *empathy* and *synchrony* — are important components of orca pod behavior. Her conclusion is based on the types of calls she hears when she is with one of the pods. One of their calls is associated more with the act of synchrony than with an activity. She has observed that the pod uses the call any time two or more of its members are doing something right together.[1]

In human behavior, synchrony is often experienced as *harmony*. Harmony is one of the themes that emerged in my research of peak experience triggered by dolphins. Although everyone with whom I spoke mentioned harmony as being an important element of their experience, one woman's story focused almost entirely on it:

My son, who was living in Nevada, called me one day and said, "There are a lot of things that I'm really mad about. I need to be able to tell you about them. But I hate to do it on the telephone." I said, "How about if I buy you an airplane ticket and you come up to Seattle and tell me face to face?" He agreed to the trip, and I made plans for us to take a whale-watching tour while he was with me. When we went out on the boat, we hadn't had "the talk" yet.

As it happened, on the day that we were on the boat, two of the orca pods that live in the waters of the San Juan Islands were meeting in the orca mating season ritual known as the superpod, so we saw an incredible amount of activity and an unusually large number of orcas. Among the pods was a mother-son pair known to locals as Slick and Mike.

> Slick and Mike started breaching [launching themselves into the air head first and falling back into the water with a splash] in tandem off the bow of the boat. Our captain, who had been taking ecotours out for twenty years, was absolutely amazed, and the woman who was with him thought it was so beautiful she began to cry. When we asked the captain and the woman why they were so excited, they said they had never before seen Slick and Mike breaching in tandem. Soon, my son and I also were in tears. We felt very much that the orcas were responding to our process. The example set by them certainly made what we were doing a lot easier. Our sharing of the experience of watching the mother-and-son orca pair made us feel like the Earth was supporting us in restoring our relationship to harmony. So that restoration was able to happen right after we got off the boat.

Dream symbology supports the hypothesis that dolphin intelligence has evolved toward an appreciation of harmony. Trisha Lamb Feuerstein reported a highly significant dream that she had in the 1970s, in which two orcas were tossing a big, soft, vinyl-covered ball back and forth between them in perfect harmony. The vinyl covering was in the form of the yin-yang symbol. She said, "I knew little about the yin-yang symbol at the time but went to the library to learn more about it." Feuerstein's research into dolphin dreams continues. At this writing, she has collected more than 50 examples of dolphins and whales overlaid on or other otherwise associated with the yin-yang symbol. "This relates to the primary themes I've found associated with them across all categories — those of harmony and balance," she reported.[2]

Dolphin cinematographer Daniel McCulloch witnessed a dolphin enactment of the yin-yang symbol of harmony in real life the first time he saw dolphins. Daniel happened to be standing on the shore of a lagoon in Hawaii, camera in hand, when two captive dolphins suddenly burst from the water. As they sailed through the air, they formed the yin-yang symbol. Daniel captured the extraordinary moment on film and the image became a widely distributed poster which he titled *Synchronicity*.

Trained observers have noticed that humans and dolphins are coevolving socially. The journals kept by Denise Herzing on the Wild Dolphin Project document a gradual shift in human-dolphin interaction dynamics. Eight years into her data collection among the dolphin populations of the Bahamas, Herzing noticed the dolphins were increasingly soliciting touch from the people who were in the water with them. In 1992, Herzing made the following entry in her journal:

The shift in the dolphins has been incredible, or our relationship at least. . . . What does it mean to have two species connect? What's in it for them? What does it mean for us? It seems like the ultimate goal of humanness is to expand our boundaries: be they personal or public, internal or external, intra or inter species. But what does it mean when another species reaches out to touch, literally and figuratively?[3]

But the shift in interspecies dynamics also created concerns for the safety of human swimmers:

. . . the dolphins were now expecting us to understand their signals and behavior, to the point of disciplining us for the wrong actions. I see this as a natural extension of our relationship and interaction. Unfortunately, I don't feel we understand the extent of what is often happening between them. For this reason, I am concerned that every human in the water be truly aware of the contextual subtleties of dolphin communication.[4]

Needing to know more about dolphins' signals for the safety of both her crew and the inexperienced volunteers she was bringing out to the Bank, Herzing made an understanding of dolphin communication and protocol one of the ongoing challenges of her research project.

Anyone who is planning to interact with dolphins owes it to themselves and the pods to acquire a working knowledge of the signs of dolphin aggression. A distressed dolphin may "shove" a human aside in the water. (Dolphins are extremely agile and precise in their movements, and displacement of a human swimmer does not occur by accident.) Repetitive head-wagging also is a sign of escalating stress and aggression, as is an "S" shaped body position — which also can indicate courtship behavior — or the lowering of head and tail while flippers are held stiffly.

It is important to be aware of signals even when not in the water, to avoid possible injury to the animal. I was once with a group of friends at the Vancouver Aquarium in British Columbia which at that time had several captive orcas on display. One of my acquaintances, Joy, had come equipped to engage in a little interspecies communication using a montage of pictures. Joy taped her colorful creation face-in on the gallery window so the tank's inhabitants could see it. Soon, one of the orcas came very close to the window and began carefully scanning the artwork. The artwork also caught the eye of the trainer, who came running into the viewing gallery in her wetsuit to warn us to remove the art from the glass if the orca showed any signs of stress. A few minutes later, the animal began to wag its head vigorously, and Joy's attempt at détente came to an end.

Captive orcas have, in isolated incidents, behaved capriciously toward their trainers, sometimes with tragic results. Years ago, when I was working as a free-lance photographer in Los Angeles, I was hired to do a photo shoot for Marineland of the Pacific. On the day I was there, I was given a peek behind the scenes at a captive orca who had committed a naughty deed — it had briefly pinned its handler to the bottom of the tank during a training session. The orca and its mate were being punished with mild sensory deprivation. The handler was hospitalized, but was recovering.

A similar but much more extreme event occurred about 13 years later, in 1991, at an entertainment park in Victoria, British Columbia. Two orcas deliberately knocked a young assistant trainer into their containment and proceeded to maul and drown her despite the attempts of bystanders to remove her from the water. The woman died before she was recovered from the tank.

Many people who see wild dolphins from a distance wonder whether the dolphins can see them in return. It was while I was collecting stories of peak experience that I realized the extent to which people underestimate dolphins' visual capabilities. Dolphins are able to use sound to convey information to each other in the low-level lighting conditions of the underwater environment, and this capability is often more useful to them than visual sight. But adaptations of the cornea and lens in the dolphin eye have given dolphins a visual acuity above water that is comparable to normal human vision in air. Underwater, dolphins are able to see better than humans. Switching between looking at objects in the water and looking at objects in the air simply requires changing the positioning of the head.

Many incidents have demonstrated how aware dolphins are of events that occur outside of the water. A wild spotted dolphin in the Bahamas mimicked one of the volunteers aboard a research vessel, presumably to demonstrate her awareness of them. It was an unusual behavior that the dolphin could not have observed elsewhere: a man on that particular expedition was wearing sargassum seaweed on his head for fun when he was aboard the boat. After a few days, the dolphin surfaced next to the boat with sargassum around her head, in obvious imitation.

The extreme range and incredible sharpness of dolphins' in-air vision was demonstrated by an event that occurred in British Columbia in 1956. Two loggers were working on a hillside. Seeing a pod of orcas below, one of the men deliberately let a log skid down the slope. The log hit an orca in the back. The animal did not seem to be seriously injured and swam away with his pod. That night, as the loggers were rowing back to their camp, the orcas suddenly reappeared and tipped the boat over. The man who had released the log vanished. The other man survived without injury.

This tragic incident illustrates the orcas' keen perception of objects on land, down to the point of discerning the subtle personal differences that distinguish two people with whom they are completely unfamiliar. It also demonstrates several aspects of the orcas' mental abilities. Not only did the orcas involved in the logging event accurately link cause and effect, the animals sought revenge in a manner that showed their ability to devise a strategy and carry it out in the future. At the same time, fairness and restraint were demonstrated — the pod's retribution was not generalized to the innocent man.

While dolphins' visual sense is excellent, their hearing and echolocation capabilities are extraordinary. The range of sound frequencies that dolphins can detect is 10 times broader than the human range. The ocean environment provides conditions that favored the development of the dolphins' sense of hearing in a way that led to the ability to hear the highest tones of any animal on Earth.[5]

Sonar, an acronym for *sound navigation and ranging,* is part of dolphins' echolocation process, but sonar is not unique to dolphins. Biosonar is used by species as diverse as cetaceans, bats, and certain types of fishes. But, of the various biosonar systems, dolphin echolocation is by far the most superbly evolved, and has served as the model for our own mechanical sonar reproduction. Biosonar still outperforms any sonar we have created. The short echolocation clicks used by dolphins encode much more information than is contained in signals of longer duration that are emitted by artificial sonar.

Dolphins are able to identify extremely small objects by projecting high-pitched clicks and then interpreting the echoes. In one classic experiment, a captive dolphin demonstrated the ability to discern the sound of a teaspoon of water being dropped into a large oceanarium pool. Each time the water dropped, the dolphin turned and directed sonar clicks precisely on the spot.

The current scientific wisdom is that dolphin sonar does not work in air, but people who spend a lot of time around dolphins sometimes venture a different opinion.

Sonar gives dolphins the capability to perceive in multiple dimensions. As a dolphin aims its head at objects, echoes are generated by the external surface of the object as well as by the object's various internal surfaces. The penetration provides dolphins with a way to gain more information than would be available from a simple, single reflection. Being extremely mobile, dolphins can direct their sonar signals on an object from many different orientations. They get slightly different bits of information from each position, and they are adept at remembering the information received from the echoes at the different positions and orientations.

Underwater, dolphins apparently perceive their environment in sound holograms, but their holographic perceptions may not be limited to sonic input. The dolphin brain has large, so-called silent areas. "Silent" means we do not know the function of those areas. I like to consider what dolphins may be capable of in the context of some extraordinary features we know about — the exceptional mental imaging capabilities possessed by a human, Temple Grandin, who has been autistic since childhood.

In *Thinking in Pictures,* Grandin described the unusual gifts for mental processing that her particular kind of autism has given her. Her mental processes are based on images that she runs and replays like a video in her mind. Her own inner world has convinced her that, contrary to prevailing scientific belief, animals do indeed have thoughts — not linear thoughts like most people, but image-based thoughts similar to her own. Grandin's description of her inner world calls attention to the likelihood that a species that has a highly developed brain and uses a sophisticated biosonar is capable of a complex mental life. In fact, with dolphins, huge brain size and a different set of external perceptions may have taken mental processing capabilities a quantum leap beyond Grandin's. Since any dolphin in a pod potentially can receive the echoes from the sonic pulses sent out by any other dolphin, pod perceptions may coalesce in a collective consciousness — the "pod mind."

In this way, the dolphin's perceptual world may be based, in part, on image-based holographics originating with the combined signals of the pod. Dolphins may even, through some other still unknown mechanism, achieve a holographic communal consciousness. Such a consciousness has been reported anecdotally for a far less sophisticated communal species by author Michael Roads, who told of a childhood experience of being lulled into the collective consciousness of a hornet hive, and of receiving communications from the hive in holographic images.[6]

The existence of a collective pod mind — especially one that could be extended to encompass humans — could help to explain a certain pod's seemingly psychic comprehension of a human death that occurred during a research expedition. The incident concerned a volunteer who died suddenly of natural causes while aboard a research vessel en route to a dolphin site. No one on board the boat had been aware that the man was having a heart problem when he excused himself and went down into the hold. The first clue occurred when the boat reached the dolphin site and found the pods acting strangely. The dolphins insisted on keeping their distance.

Just then, the man's daughter discovered him dead in his bunk.

The project leader became convinced the dolphins had sensed something was wrong before anyone on board knew. Just as peculiarly, she noted, when the boat headed back to port, the dolphins escorted them as they often did, but not in the usual manner of riding the bow wave. Instead, they flanked the boat at a distance of 50 feet. When the research vessel returned to the site two days later with the same group on board, the pod's behavior was once again normal.

In the context of our present knowledge about the senses, perception, and information exchange, an incident such as occurred aboard the research vessel defies comprehension. What is known is that in the presence of dolphins, no secrets can be kept about emotions or anatomy. When a dolphin scans another flesh-and-blood being with its sonar, it receives echoes from interior as well as exterior surfaces. Racing pulse, upset stomach, tumors — everything becomes communal knowledge. What dolphins perceive when they scan another creature must be similar to what we humans see in the hospital laboratory during an ultrasound test, as we watch the ghostly internal images throbbing with life on the diagnostician's viewing screen.

Dolphin handlers who supervise the public in dolphin encounters have many humorous stories about the interest that dolphins take in swimmers who have implants. A trainer at a facility which offers public swims with captive dolphins told me that their dolphins often cluster around a swimmer who has an interesting internal feature such as a hip implant or a fetus. In the latter case, if the pregnancy is in an early stage, the woman may not yet know she is pregnant, so the dolphins may be giving her an important cue. Once, the trainer said, a dolphin was seen scanning a man's chest at close range. Then the dolphin swam away, got the attention of another dolphin, and brought the other dolphin back with him to the man. Both dolphins began scanning the man's chest. Later, when the man left the water, he told the trainer he had a heart valve implant. The trainer recalled, "It was as if the first dolphin had told the second dolphin, 'Hey, I've found something really interesting. Come look at this.'" This capability has provided part of the basis for the dolphins' emerging reputation as healers.

4

Why Dolphins?

. . . is the unconditional love that many have reported experiencing when swimming with [dolphins] the secret of the dolphin's healing powers? How important is the release of pent-up emotions? . . . Does the dolphin set up the beneficial energy fields that some researchers in the United States see as crucial to the proper functioning of the nervous system and of the brain?
Are dolphins in some way telepathic?
Do the ultra-sonic sounds they produce stimulate the release of endorphins? . . .
Are there even more possibilities?

Horace Dobbs

While the U.S. Navy was exploring the potential of using dolphins in military operations, the American public was becoming acquainted with dolphins through an Atlantic bottlenose dolphin performer, Flipper, who was actually a succession of dolphins. At about the same time, other adult dolphins who were contemporaries of the Flippers were caught in the wild and readied for a traveling show. But before the dolphins could be put on the road, Betsy Smith, a professor of social work at Florida International University, happened to see divers interacting with them. Intrigued, she put her neurologically impaired brother in the pool, and discovered that the dolphins were very effective in breaking through the emotional wall that isolates such children. Next, she brought a few autistic children over to the facility for a swim. Again, as with her brother, the dolphins' consistent spontaneity and ability to read the subtleties of aberrant human behavior produced promising results. Road show plans were scuttled in favor of a dolphin-assisted therapy program.

In time, other similar facilities opened in the Florida Keys. The Atlantic bottlenose dolphin's tractability and adaptability to captivity has made it the dolphin of choice for therapy, as it was for John Lilly's language studies. But the broader scientific community has never become convinced about the effectiveness of dolphin-assisted therapy. A 1996 *New Age Journal* article about dolphins and healing quoted Smith as saying that popular, unproven applications were muddying the research waters. The article cited her concerns about "practitioners who attribute near mystical powers to the animals. 'People who will sell you dolphin dreaming may well be the same ones who once sold you EST, or North American Indian sweat lodges,' . . . ." The same article also quoted Ric O'Barry, a well-known dolphin activist, discrediting dolphins' fabled power to heal: "The dolphin is the new age unicorn . . . . If you believe that it works, it will work for you. You can accomplish the same thing with a puppy if you go to the pound."[1]

In actuality, little basis exists for equating the healing effect of a swim with a dolphin with the effects of cuddling a puppy. True, a person who strokes a domesticated animal tends to be calmed and soothed. By contrast, with dolphins, pacification comes as the result of eye contact rather than touch, and the human's pulse is likely to race during the encounter, revealing a state of excitement, not calm. Yet, the outcome is similar — reduction in stress occurs. This is part of the paradox of dolphins as healers.

Dolphins are known as innovative performers, spontaneously making up new behaviors that keep an audience amused and ensuring a steady stream of fish reinforcements from their trainers. A performing dog isn't capable of such sophisticated behavior — the performance would have to be carefully rehearsed. A dog's behavior is stereotypic, which means the dog has a limited number of behavior repertoires. It is dolphins who are our matches or, perhaps, even our superiors, for many trainers and researchers who work with dolphins have discovered that as they experiment with and attempt to manipulate the dolphins, the dolphins are experimenting with and manipulating them.

A humorous story involving one of the dolphins in John Lilly's study illustrates the dolphins' ability to mete out manipulation in return. Hoping to film a dolphin rescuing a human, Lilly staged a mock drowning by having one of his assistants go into the water and pretend to be in distress. The dolphin, Sissy, swam over to the "victim" and pushed him to the side of the pool. But, then, the drowning episode had to be reenacted because Lilly had forgotten to remove the cap from the camera lens. So, the assistant returned to the water and again feigned distress. That time, however, Sissy recognized the deception. Instead of rescuing the man, she beat him up.

In therapy, flexible behavior is demonstrated as the ability to challenge the patient in innovative ways. In this regard, dolphins have shown themselves to be highly effective as adjuncts in emotional healing work. In the United States, dolphin-assisted therapy is most often applied to benefit children. Dolphins are used with autistic children, Downs syndrome patients, and young people with emotional problems. They also have alleviated severe chronic depression in adults.

Ambiguity exists concerning the use of animals of any species as healers, because, in conventional animal-assisted work, therapy cases are idiosyncratic — that is, no two of them are alike. The uncertainties are compounded by the fact that long-term follow-up is usually not possible. As a result, the outcomes for both animal-assisted and dolphin-assisted therapy are uncertain, and attempts at establishing statistical proof have not yet satisfied the scientific community within the United States.

In Russia, however, dolphin-assisted therapy is considered a legitimate healing tool. A marine mammal center in Sevastopol, Ukraine, that is a former military base has continued to maintain its dolphins by using them to treat hundreds of illnesses. In its first seven years of operation, the facility saw more than 2,000 patients, and 96 percent of them reportedly experienced some improvement. Among patients under age seven, the rate of cure for neuroses was 70 percent. Marine center therapists and dolphins are successfully treating a variety of conditions, including neuroses ranging from stuttering to obsessive disorder and deafness in children. (Commenting on the enormous difference in the skill levels required of the dolphins in the work before and after the end of the Cold War, one of their veteran navy trainers said, "It's like asking a top designer who has made aircraft all his life to make a bicycle.")[2]

It is highly unlikely that peak experience is a factor in dolphin-assisted therapy involving children, because children do not have the cognitive development that is required to experience a peak.

During the time I was a member of the Dream A Dolphin Foundation's scientific committee, I and other committee members were concerned with identifying the variables that could be influencing the outcomes of dolphin-assisted therapy. In one brainstorming exercise, we had identified more than 80 variables. Several years later, Nichola Webb, a clinical psychologist in Perth, Australia, saw my published research findings concerning peak experience, and contacted me. She wanted me to know that she had just completed a study of the effects of swimming with dolphins who were contained in sea pens. This was the kind of baseline information that our committee would have found useful. She introduced herself to me in an e-mail that said, in part,

---

> The area has struck a deep chord within me since I commenced the research in 1996 and I was (and still am) keen to place a scientific slant on such important work so that others within the skeptical science field may come to realize the great benefits of this therapy. My work was not easy to start with as you may not be surprised to learn. Psychology academics were not initially supportive and similar researchers were difficult to find. This made me more determined than ever to persist with the research. It took me three years of endless legwork before an end result was seen.

A year later, Nichola published a paper describing her work.[3] I was excited about what she had accomplished and what it meant for the study of the therapeutic effects of human-dolphin interactions. Working with the essences of the experience, I had introduced the human-animal interaction community to the psycho-spiritual dimensions of the human-dolphin interaction. Now, Nichola's efforts provided a different kind of proof. Between her published research and mine, human sciences-based studies into interactions with dolphins were finally getting some attention in the scientific community. Not only did Nichola gather self-assessments from her human participants regarding their feelings of psychological and physiological well-being and anxiety before and after swimming with dolphins, in order to compare the effects of swimming *without* dolphins present, she also had collected information from people who had come to the beach merely to swim.[4]

Among Nichola's interesting discoveries were the following observations: First, ratings of well-being were higher in people who swam with dolphins than in those who swam just in water. This rating pattern held not only after the swims, but before the swims as well. She also learned that people who were about to swim with dolphins rated themselves as feeling more energetic and positive than those who were anticipating only a routine ocean swim. Putting together these two pieces of information, she speculated that the heightened sense of well-being was the result of the person's anticipation of a positive experience.

She also pointed out that the increase in well-being after swimming, either with or without dolphins, is consistent with Lilly's Water Flotation Theory, put forth by John Lilly, one of the first dolphin researchers. The theory states that immersion in water at a comfortable temperature induces states of relaxation and increased well-being. Muscular tension and blood pressure decreases, and the brain enters a state of consciousness similar to meditation.

Many people who swim with dolphins report experiencing a stimulating effect on their heart as a result of the animals' presence. They sometimes describe this effect as an "opening of the heart." But few people are aware that a close connection exists between heart harmonics and synchronization of the brain's right and left hemispheres. Simeon Nartoomid, a Santa Fe man who is a certified HeartMath practitioner, became aware of the dolphins' effect on both heart and brain during his first in-water experience with a wild pod:

> I started calling to the pod through my heart energies. Within a few minutes the dolphins surfaced around me. I could hear and feel their sonar in my chest cavity — a pleasant experience that seemed to "open me up," for I felt a distinct shift in my awareness and then seemed able to understand these beings more fully.
>
> The next day I went for another swim, and again was surrounded by dozens of spinner dolphins. The pods, which varied in size from two to 12 animals, came as close as four feet away, and they were looking at me. The energy I experienced from them was incredible. Their sonar sounds seemed to penetrate every cell of my body. I started to "see" rainbow hues in the central cortex of my brain, in the area near the pituitary gland.

As a result of this experience, Simeon concluded that proximity to dolphins can efficiently entrain a human's brainwaves to their own brainwave forms. His conclusion is validated by research conducted by the AquaThought Foundation, which charted some of the changes that take place in the human brain when it is entrained to dolphin waveforms.[5] Dolphins were found to have the effect of promoting alpha brainwave activity, which in humans contributes to the creation of a calmer, more receptive state of mind and also enhances immune system functioning. Alpha is the desired background state for biofeedback, accelerated learning, and stress reduction techniques.[6]

Simeon's rainbow-hued side effects sound spectacular, and I have heard of other similarly spectacular effects. Being on the receiving end of a dolphin sonic scan apparently can produce a variety of dramatic physical phenomena. Some swimmers have reported a sensation like an electrical current or buzz, or a generalized sensation that sounds like a creaky door and travels all the way up and down one side of their body. One woman reported an extraordinary experience that involved a dolphin who wasn't even close to her. At the time the incident occurred, she was in the pool and the dolphin was about 15 feet away. Suddenly, an area on her head about the size of a quarter seemed to explode. "*Fwwoom.*" The effect was so loud she seemed to be hearing thunder or clashing cymbals. She also felt a cracking effect and was temporarily blinded. "It was the most extraordinary sensation I've ever felt in my life," she said. An after-effect lingered for days.

The release of endorphins may be one of the factors that contribute to the healing nature of the dolphin's presence. Theories also exist about sound. Olivia DeBergerac, an Australian dolphin researcher and sound therapist, believes that dolphin sounds help us to shift our brains into a new consciousness. In her book *The Dolphin Within,* she points out that although much of the sound made by dolphins is outside the range of our auditory hearing, we still feel their entire range of acoustics throughout our bodies. She cites the work of Alfred Tomatis, a French medical doctor who found that prenatal brain development is influenced by the sounds the fetus hears while in the womb.

To the unborn infant, whose hearing is five times more acute than it will be in air, sounds are experienced predominantly as high-pitched squeaks, hisses, swishes, and whistles, DeBergerac says. That frequency range lies well beyond our normal in-air sound spectrum but overlaps with dolphins' ultra-high-pitched frequency range. DeBergerac believes dolphin sound is an effective therapy because of its similarity to the rhythmic booming of the human mother's circulatory system as heard by the unborn child.

In transformational encounters, particularly those involving wild dolphins, the dolphin sometimes is perceived as seeking out the human and initiating interaction. Might dolphins used in therapeutic interactions likewise be engaging in healing activities intentionally, as some practitioners claim?

The scientists who are investigating the question of dolphins as intentional healers have not, to date, found any hard evidence that in the process of emitting a variety of sounds, the dolphin intentionally directs its biosonar therapeutically. During one study, however, when a patient was held in a floating position during interactions with a captive dolphin, the dolphin took a position so that the area within the animal's skull (known as the *melon*) that focuses and amplifies the sonar was just behind the patient's skull. In that position, a dolphin would be able to project sound directly into a patient's brain.[7]

Ric O'Barry's comparison of dolphins and puppies as healers reminds me of one of the first questions I asked when I began exploring the dolphins' role in healing, and that was how other species compare with dolphins in therapeutic situations. I eventually had the opportunity to discuss this matter with Mother Hildegard George, the Ph.D. and child psychologist who introduced animals into psychotherapy. Mother Hildegard has been associated with Green Chimneys, the premier animal-assisted therapy program center, located in New York state. She has never worked with dolphins, but she has used a variety of animals in therapeutic situations. She gave me her professional opinion about comparative intelligence and suitability of the large mammals most frequently used in animal-assisted therapy, including the dolphin:

> GOATS: Absolutely wonderful — very gregarious, easy to train, much easier to work with than sheep, and they love to be in the fray of things. HORSES: Not as intelligent as many people think, and not as intelligent as some of the other mammals used in therapy. In order to be used in therapy with children, a horse needs considerably more training than a large mammal like a llama. That's why most of the horses used in therapy are older. My 4-H kids train 7-month-old llamas to work on a halter in a matter of hours. We couldn't accomplish that so quickly with a horse. So with horses, effectiveness in therapy may be related not so much to the animal's intelligence as to the amount of training it has had. LLAMAS: In addition to their intelligence, in therapy situations llamas offer the advantage of being unusual. DOLPHINS: There is something special about using dolphins in therapy. They're a lot closer to us than any other animal. They're smartest, they're capable

of a sensing at a level beyond other animals, and they're the closest to us in communication capabilities. ORCAS: A very intelligent being, very sensitive to humans. (Orcas are never used in therapy, but they are indigenous to the waters of the San Juan Islands, where Mother Hildegard lives.)

Of the various large and small species that are used in animal-assisted therapy, dogs have the most similarities with humans. It is the dogs, with their rituals of greeting and subservience that are so readily recognizable in the context of our human cultures, who win our ready acceptance as surrogate kin. The transpersonal psychologist Ken Wilber explains the similarities in terms of *shared emotional world space.* We have a lot of emotional resonance with dogs but much less with cats, which is probably why some people prefer dogs to cats. We also happen to have a considerable amount of emotional resonance with dolphins, judging from our reactions to them. But, unlike the human-dolphin relationship, the human-dog relationship is based on dominance, and that hierarchy changes the dynamics and qualities of the interspecies interaction.

Domesticated dogs are bred to maintain puppylike qualities into adulthood, a characteristic called *neoteny*. In this way and through other related animal husbandry practices, all of the domesticated species have been altered from their wild progenitors over many generations of psychological domination and genetic manipulation. Part of the price the animal pays for domestication is a certain amount of marginalization and diminishment in human eyes. A puppy or dog may be treated with abundant affection, but that affection is part of our patronization of the animal. In return, subservience is expected and usually demanded — as, in fact, it should be. We must maintain our edge over a dog as it matures because the dog views its human as the replacement for that pack member which in its normal species social unit would be the leader.

Gregory Bateson, a well-known anthropologist of John Lilly's era, explained the reversal of hierarchy that occurs in human-dolphin interactions compared with household animals: "A dog or cat . . . puts you in the position of parent or leader . . . . [but] when you are in the water with a porpoise, you are the child and the porpoise is the parent."[8]

Bateson's observations were directed at techniques for learning about the animal, but the hierarchical difference he pointed out also has implications for human-dolphin encounters in general. We relate to dolphins in an entirely different way than we relate to dogs, and those differences affect each species' role in healing.

In addition, a dolphin is a wild animal. In native American cultures, the animals that are most subservient — the domesticated species and especially dogs — are the least respected, while the wild animals, because of their differences, are accorded the greatest respect. The American shaman Michael Harner has noted that regardless of culture, humans feel a particularly strong emotional connection with wild animal alter egos. For this reason alone, the wild species, and especially exotic species like the dolphin, possess charisma and can engage us in ways that our domesticated companions cannot.

In asking, in effect, "Why dolphins? Why not puppies?" Ric O'Barry is not the only person to raise that kind of challenge. Several years after O'Barry's statement appeared in the *New Age Journal*, a scientist trained in the physical sciences put a new twist on the question by asking me, "Why dolphins? Why not bison?" He was, he hastened to assure me, a man of the seas; his field is oceanography. (This bit of background was evidently offered to let me know he likes dolphins and is generally inclined to see things in their favor.) But, all the same, he clearly took no stock in dolphins' fabled abilities.

The oceanographer's question actually brings a different response than the animal activist's question, in that the two species that are being compared are wild, and both represent mammals not often encountered by the average person. Bison have an advantage over dogs in terms of being unusual, but owing to the quirks of evolution, bison are not aquatic. Nor do they emanate the ultrasonic clicks or energy fields that affect human physiology, and that fact brings to mind the one nonaquatic creature possessing an important trait in common with the dolphin — the bat. The bat utilizes ultrasonics much as the dolphin does. Yet, healing, communication, or, for that matter, mystical experience, is no more commonplace with bats than it is with bison or with puppies. So, a more appropriate question would be, *Why dolphins but not bats?*

One aspect of the wild-animal-triggered peak experience that has fascinated me for several years involves the question of how experiences with the dolphins contrast with experiences involving the great apes. Both species rank high within the animal kingdom by the human-centered standards we apply to animal intelligence (actually, the dolphin scores higher than the chimpanzee — see Chapter 3). Yet, each species has arrived at its advanced mental state by radically different paths. In contrast to the dolphins, whose evolutionary divergence can be traced in the fossil records back at least 30 million years, the primates are relatively late arrivals on the planet.

The first monkeylike creatures seem to have appeared in the trees no longer than 25 million years ago. The advent of the great apes, to which our human lineage owes its origins, occurred even more recently. The great apes have been on the planet six to nine million years. Our own predecessors became a distinct presence on the planet within the last six million years, so recently that the DNA of other offshoots of the great ape lineage, the chimpanzees and bonobos, still differs from our own DNA by just a couple of percentage points. Many people visit the great apes in their exotic habitats, just as people are increasingly seeking out wild dolphins. Yet, in our folk wisdom, the great apes are never touted as being more intelligent than we are. Although certain gorillas and chimpanzees have demonstrated an amazing benevolence and compassion toward humans under extenuating circumstances, no one is calling them *healers* or *ascended masters,* two terms that are frequently applied to dolphins by some of the dolphins' more spiritual admirers. Of all the species, the dolphins stand apart for consistently triggering ultraordinary, transcendent experience.

In the realm of peak experience involving animals, the one other formal study that has been conducted focuses on the great apes. The researcher is an experimental psychologist. An acquaintance told me about the work of Anthony Rose, and when I called Rose to introduce myself and my research, he was as surprised to learn about what I was doing as I had been to learn about him. His reports on the subject have been presented mostly within the context of primatology conferences rather than published in indexed scientific journals, so I had not found references in any of the database searches which any scientist or scholar routinely conducts as the foundation for investigating a research question.

Rose doesn't apply the term *peak experience* to his studies or draw upon the extensive literature of classical peak experience in interpreting his results, as I did. He calls the events *profound interspecies encounters.* The encounters he describes do involve epiphanies, or are cross-culturally enlightening, or in other ways engender interspecies trust. But none of them engages the elated emotions, as the dolphin-triggered peak does.

Yet, certain commonalities exist between the dolphin-triggered peak experience and Rose's descriptions of profound interspecies encounters. In the wild, both species are encountered in exotic locales — the dolphins, in the open ocean or river; the chimpanzees, in remote jungles. Chimps may form bonds with the tourists, and they may even be "adopted" by humans as part of a preservation program, just as dolphins may. Also with either species, people who have a positive experience in the wild usually return home with an increased sense of advocacy. Rose said,

---

> those epiphanies that are characterized as scientific and naturalistic by their reporters have a central humanistic component. The discoveries and realizations that move us most, that we never forget, always seem to tell us something personally important about ourselves and our kinship with the other animals.[9]

Rose also has given extensive consideration to the impact that a "dangerous, distant, or disinterested" animal can have on us when it surprises us by seeking a friendly encounter. Although Rose doesn't use the term *transformational* in connection with profound interspecies events, he does say they are life-changing because they put us on a fast track back to Nature.

The first zoo director to receive a captive dolphin described the animal as having "twinkling eyes." The creature was, he declared, "so new, strange and extremely weird" that it looked more like a bewitched being than a mammal.[10] The zoo director's remarks bring up an important point regarding our perceptions about dolphins. We can hardly avoid anthropomorphizing — that is, interpreting the animal's behavior in terms of human behavior and human attributes — when we encounter a primate. By contrast, the dolphin is so different from humans that we would expect little of ourself to be reflected in it either biologically or behaviorally. Yet, many people discover a surprising degree of richness and depth in the experience of encountering a dolphin either in captivity or in the wild.

By reflecting upon our perceptions of these two very different nonhuman species — dolphin and primate — and also upon the similarities that exist between humans and dolphins despite major evolutionary differences, we can better understand and appreciate the dolphins' ability to serve as mirrors.

Not only do the dolphins offer the opportunity to connect more strongly with elusive aspects of our human self, that connection is made as we go beyond the boundaries of our normal cultural experience and enter into the world of another species. In this way, we are not only learning more about the interspecies edge, we also are bridging it.

5

Entering Into Dolphin Consciousness

Each spring, on exactly the same dates, millions of dolphins are said to converge in a huge, spiraling superpod at a certain location in the tepid waters of Indonesia. No human knows the reason for the dolphins' 4-day convocation or understands the mechanism behind its precise timing, inspiring Dan Furst to write, "Would it not be interesting to send one or more boats of humans and other animals to the periphery of the event, and ask the dolphins' permission to participate as observers?"

After Dan Furst's Universal Festival Calendar

In the province of the mind, what one believes to be true is true or becomes true ... In the mind, there are no limits.

John Lilly

The Maori people of New Zealand have a saying, "If a dolphin comes to you in a dream, it was not a dream. The dolphin has really come."

I have noticed that people who are drawn to the dolphins often have had dolphins appear to them in their dreams. The connection may also occur in reverse. When someone signs up for one of my dolphin encounter groups, I suggest to them that they may want to start watching their dreams. Dolphin replicas and images also may begin appearing to them synchronistically on television or billboards, in books, and in other ways. All of these events are indications of a *waking dream* — a dream that continues in a series of synchronicities after the dreamer is awake.[1] Such experiences have the effect of an invitation to begin the journey toward dolphin consciousness.

In the first dream about dolphins that I can recall having, *An orca riding so high in the water that I can see its broad back and curving dorsal fin swims up to me and nudges the palm of my hand with the tip of its snout. Chris Peknic is there, too; we are standing together waist-deep in the water.*

"Have the dolphins ever come to you holographically?" a friend from my circle of dolphin people asked me. "No, never," I quickly replied. But later, I realized that they had come to me in just that way during a trip to Hawaii when I was lying on the beach after a morning of swimming in the ocean: *Pleasantly drained by my hour in the water, I am drifting between sleep and wakefulness. Suddenly, I see a pod of half a dozen dolphins swimming toward me. Inwardly, I welcome them.* When I was again fully awake, I found myself wondering if these same dolphins actually swim in the sea.

Months later, the dolphin image reemerged while I was sitting quietly in a meditation retreat: *A vision of a joyous, leaping dolphin arcing through the air intrudes suddenly upon my inner world.*

In my most vivid dream about dolphins and whales, *I am driving northward along the east coast of Vancouver Island in British Columbia. Offshore, dozens, perhaps even hundreds, of humpback whales and orcas are swimming, all headed in the same direction as I am going and not far from shore. Somehow, I am seeing them in their full form, not just as fins and humps on the surface the way someone on land normally would view a whale. Although I am in one sense on land, it is also as if I am already in the blue-green water with them. They seem within reach, just yards away. I want to swim to them, but I am concerned about being carried away into the straits by the swirling currents. I consider ways in which I might secure a lifeline to myself.*

For many people, a dolphin dream becomes a waking dream. I am among the growing number of people who are living the waking dream of the dolphins, and, in that way, connecting with the dolphin archetype.

There are many ways of experiencing the archetypes and incubating a waking dream. While I was still in the early stages of exploring the human-dolphin connection from the perspective of peak experience, Chris Peknic was becoming interested in breathwork, in part because of the vivid dreaming and archetypes it invokes.

In one of its most carefully structured practices, breathwork is a technique of conscious breathing developed by Stanislav Grof, the author of numerous books including *The Psychology of the Future.* In almost any form, breathwork involves three- to four-hour sessions during which the participant breathes a little deeper and faster than usual. Evocative music is used to facilitate the release of emotions. Skilled facilitators create and maintain a safe environment in which the participants can freely experience nonordinary states of consciousness.

With his wife Judy, who is a clinical psychologist and long-time Vipassana meditator, Chris began studying the breathwork techniques developed by Grof. Chris quickly saw that breathwork could be applied to facilitate wild dolphin swim programs. His goal became to combine dolphin encounter seminars with meditative and breathwork experiences.

In a statement about the application of breathwork within the context of the work of The Dolphin Institute, Chris later wrote,

---

> Holotropic Breathwork is one of a number of techniques that have been applied through human history to achieve an expanded, nonordinary consciousness. Among the other approaches that have achieved similar results are deep meditation, dreams, and shamanic rituals. The goal of each of these modes for expanding consciousness is to work toward retaining the same connection or feeling of oneness later, after we have returned to our everyday state of awareness.
>
> Breathwork is simple both in theory and practice. By utilizing the breath in a slightly different, more effective manner, we can increase our state of awareness and consciousness. We begin to experience the present moment instead of living in the past and the future. The opening up that occurs is part of the process of dropping our everyday armor and letting go of petty concerns. As we concentrate on our breath, the veil that normally blocks us from experiencing an expanded state begins to lift. With the expansion of consciousness, we experience emotions, feelings, and new states of being, and our human-centered per-

spective subsides. At the same time, we achieve a stronger sense of connection with the universal consciousness — that sense of something much larger than ourself. I believe that by enhancing our breathing processes and expanding our consciousness prior to, during, and after free-dolphin swim encounters, we can increase our capability for making a significant connection with the dolphins.

Breathwork also enables us to better access the knowledge held by the intuitive right side of our brain, and to integrate that knowledge with the knowledge of the logical left side of our brain. In this regard, breathwork is unique among the modes used to evoke altered consciousness, because it involves a dynamic the dolphins have mastered.

Because of the powerful experiences breathwork can evoke, breathing exercises of this kind should be done only under the supervision of professionals specifically trained for such explorations, and in the context of a safe and knowledgeably managed program.

When I present a combined breathwork and swim or dolphin-watch seminar, I structure the program to give participants the option of participating in a formal breathwork session both before and after entering the water. By preparing for dolphins in this way, we can increase our awareness on both scientific and experiential levels. I believe that by taking this approach, we are enhancing our ability to have a positive influence on the other creatures who share our planet.

(For a full presentation about dolphin breathing and the rationale underlying Chris's approach, see his essays, "The Equality of Human and Dolphin" and "Exploring the Breath," in the Addendum.)

Like Chris, I believe that there is something special about the dolphin's breathing. To listen to the dolphin's sharp, *whooshing* exhalation is like listening to the heartbeat of another human. For me, the sound of the dolphins' breathing seems to evoke a primal memory. One of my most memorable experiences in the ocean is an experience of dolphin breathing that occurred during an encounter group. We had all regrouped onboard for a lunch break. After we had eaten and everyone was resting, Virginia Lee, a commercial director from Los Angeles, suddenly asked me, "Do you feel like going for a swim?" I am always happy to get back in the water, so the two of us put on our fins and masks and slipped in. After we were a considerable distance from the boat, we noticed several dolphins swimming on the surface of the water not far from where we were.

Npui. Npui. Npui.

We could hear their exhalations and see the vapor of their breaths. They were alternately swimming in circles and then darting in straight lines. Sometimes they would head straight toward us, and then, when they were just a few yards away, they would abruptly change course again. But they never left the surface.

Npui. Npui. Npui.

Virginia and I treaded water and craned our necks. "Can you see what they are doing?" I finally asked her.

"They seem to be jostling."

Npui. Npui. Npui.

The captain signaled us to return to the boat just then. But I am sure we both would have been happy to remain where we were, bobbing in mid-ocean, in the dolphins' element, for as long as that trio remained there. We had been privileged to look through a rare window onto the private life of the pod, made possible only because at that time, they were neither interested in nor disturbed by our presence. It is the closest I have yet come to feeling, for a few precious minutes, like a part of the dolphins' world. I sometimes think back to that time in the water and the sound the dolphins made as they breathed. To me, *npui* seems like an oceanic mantra, and the breathing of the dolphin sounds like the breathing of the universe.

Intentionally or coincidentally, the dolphins are giving us wonderful gifts like joy, peace, love, and courage. In return, we can ask, "What should we be doing for the dolphins?" One answer to this question is that we can take responsibility for the animals' natural environment and their treatment as individuals and pods — perhaps one of the most important aspects of entering into dolphin consciousness because it is not self-serving. Heightened environmental awareness is a sign of advancement beyond a human-centered perspective, and it also is one of the typical outcomes of a significant dolphin encounter. People whose first encounters with dolphins occur in captive situations often see the need to bring captivity to an end, acquire a heightened ecological world-view, and become activists on behalf of the dolphins. The cultivation of the dream dolphin and dolphin archetype through breathwork and attention to our dreams also helps people to achieve these realizations.

Although most of the people who are helped by the dolphins are more interested in results than reasons, acquiring a scientific understanding of the dolphins' unique effects on us will benefit society. Every bit of understanding that we can acquire about the influence that animals, domesticated and wild, have on our human consciousness will help us to transform our society toward an interspecies world-view. The time has come for such a transformation to occur. The study of consciousness is being hailed as the next great area of scientific advancement in the new century, just at the time when humankind seems due for our species' next major evolutionary step.

If there is a next step beyond *Homo sapiens,* will we step toward the shadow or toward the light? Bioethicist Michael Fox envisions both possibilities. One of his visions — the dark one — is of *Homo technos,* technocratic man, a creature who will exploit all of life and turn the natural world into a humanized and industrialized technosphere. His second vision represents the light: *Homo pansapiens,* a being who embodies compassion and reverence for all of Creation. Futurist Barbara Marx Hubbard speaks with conviction of *Homo universalis,* a universal humanity that is coevolutionary and cocreative with Creation itself. Mystic Richard Moss does not suggest a new species name when he speaks of humanity's constantly expanding emotional repertoire, which he says is a hallmark of our species' evolution in consciousness. Scholar Jürgen Kremer points out that evolution is not necessarily a linear event, and that our concept of it should not reflect only the values of Western culture. Rather, he says, evolution moves in cycles and spirals, and we must view it in a way that allows a return to our indigenous roots.

The rock art of Australia, some of which is 40,000 years old, includes an ancient cave painting that shows a human coming out of the blowhole of a dolphin. Kremer's perspectives on the evolution of consciousness provide a scientific context for the folk myth of man as the dream of the dolphin. His perspective is compatible with the teachings of theologist Pierre Teilhard de Chardin, who concluded that humanity is headed toward unification into a single interthinking group—in essence, the creation of a supermind for the planet. However, because of our indoctrination since birth in the concept that humans are supreme on the planet, we must be aware of two caveats concerning the way we approach the supermind concept. The first caveat concerns our human-centered tendency to view our species' evolutionary path in different terms than we consider the evolutionary paths of other species. For most of us, the extinction of another species, although an unfortunate event, is imaginable and, ultimately, acceptable. We are not inclined to dwell upon thoughts of our own species' extinction, just as we do not (and possibly cannot) imagine our own demise. It is from this perspective that we envision glorious hypothetical next steps such as those proposed by Hubbard and Teilhard de Chardin. Yet, there is another perspective on evolution offered by Michael Fox in *One Earth, One Mind* that is panspecies:

> [Evolution] has no real direction or final goal. . . . No species has a particular purpose other than to survive, adapt, and procreate. No species is more — or less — important than another . . . [4]

My second caveat concerns human-centered thought. We should not make the mistake of defining the noosphere — that vast, interthinking group mind proposed by Teilhard de Chardin — in a way that excludes other consciousnesses such as the cetacean mind. In fact, the noosphere may already exist, brought into being by the collective minds of the whales.

Yet another evolutionary possibility exists for humans, and this one encompasses dolphins. After evolving alongside one of the largest brains on the planet for millions of years, we may be on a converging course with it. Our next evolutionary leap may be the transformation of some members of our species into *Homo delphinus* — human-dolphin.

6

Homo Delphinus, Human-Dolphin

I want humanity to know that living inside every human, there's an aquatic soul. It's going to give a whole new kind of hope to the world.

Francisco Ferraras

A few scientists have seriously proposed that the primate lineage from which we humans branched off was at one time partially aquatic. Now, in humanity's collective conscious, a mythology is emerging to point us back to the ocean — the mythology of *Homo delphinus,* a new species of human, literally, human-dolphin. Though the species is new, the concept is as old as humankind. A close relationship between humans and dolphins is portrayed in the mythologies of many cultures, starting with the oldest culture of all, that of the Australian aborigines. In certain tribes of contemporary Australian aborigines, the mythology of a shared ancestry between humans and dolphins lives on, and some aborigines continue to retain their traditional belief in the transmigration of souls between humans and dolphins.

The Chumash Indians also have a human-dolphin creation mythology. When their ancestors came to California from their original home in the South Pacific, they traveled on a rainbow bridge. During the journey, some of the people looked down into the ocean, and, becoming dizzy, fell into the water, where they were turned into dolphins by their protector-goddess.

Among the growing number of people in Western culture who are feeling called by the dolphins are some who believe themselves to be dolphins in human form. This belief, which is reminiscent of the indigenous peoples' traditions, is now emerging even among children, some of whom become aware of their cetacean connection through dreams. Jeremy Taylor, a professional dream worker, is among those who have noticed dolphins appearing increasingly in childrens' dreams. "I have met one young lad who dreams of dolphins so often that he is convinced he is a reincarnated dolphin, coming back in human form to do something about the human decimation of the wild dolphin population," Taylor told me.

Jeremy Taylor also knows several children who have developed a similar conviction about being reincarnated whales. It will be interesting to see if children who hold such beliefs continue to retain them when they are adults, and, if they do, how it will influence their lives.

The former Soviet Union is the cradle of the reemergence in modern culture of the *Homo delphinus* mythology. From there, word of a new kind of aquatic human has spread to other parts of the industrialized world — myths of babies and children who live in the water. These children are said to sleep on the bottoms of swimming pools and come up for air about once in every six minutes, dolphinlike. Yet, no references to *Homo delphinus* are to be found in the scientific journals. Nor do the journals mention dolphin midwifery, which is a folk practice.

Homo delphinus and dolphin midwifery converged as the result of modern-day birthing practices in the Black Sea, where Igor Charkovsky, a Soviet midwife, happened to be experimenting with underwater birthing techniques. Charkovsky observed that dolphins have an affinity with the unborn child. Charkovsky watched dolphins gather around the women who were about to give birth, and he noticed that the dolphins sometimes participated in the process by nuzzling the newborn babies to the surface. The mothers seemed to gain a sense of protection and safety from the dolphins' presence. Charkovsky extended his birthing practices to include dolphins and soon was convinced that the new approach yielded long-term benefits. Babies born in the presence of dolphins were said to be extraordinary children with IQs over 150, extremely stable emotional bodies, and unusually strong physical bodies. He claimed that the dolphins' powerful biofield affects the mothers and infants, an effect that is enhanced as seawater accumulates and facilitates the transmission of the bioenergy. In Charkovsky's paradigm, the dolphins' biofield creates an optimal environment, an environment that offered the best conditions imaginable for a child's development, and, by extension, for the development of humanity.

The prospects sound appealing, even exciting. Yet, the world media have cast a skeptical eye on Charkovsky's activities and discredited him. *The New York Times* exposed Charkovsky's water birthing methods as serving to increase the baby's endurance rather than to reduce the pain and stress of the birthing process.[1] The article did not mention dolphins, nor are dolphins present in any of the video footage I have seen showing Charkovsky with his patients. The *Times'* article focused instead on Charkovsky's radical techniques, including ice water dips for the newborns. Delivery was followed immediately with swimming exercises, which were part of the regimen that Charkovsky used to produce superbabies. The *Times* revealed that despite the title of "doctor" given to Charkovsky by his clients, he is what is known as a spiritual midwife, meaning that he is not a medical doctor and has had no formal obstetrical training. Eventually, Charkovsky was censured by the authorities in his homeland. He emigrated to the United States and now lives in Madison, Wis.

Nevertheless, Charkovsky has become legendary in the circles of humans who love dolphins. The Soviet dolphin-assisted birthing experiments were conducted at Moscow University in a large tank. Soviet researchers are said to have placed three dolphins in attendance with every pregnant woman as she went into labor. One dolphin tended the mother, one tended the infant, and one tended the space, just as occurs in a dolphin pod.[2]

Dolphin-assisted birthing has never been legal in the United States, but experiments have been carried out in other parts of the world. In 1992, health care professional John Float assisted British obstetrician Gowri Motha on a birthing project at a Red Sea facility. John says the mothers-to-be were allowed to swim and interact with dolphins, and to receive dolphins' high-frequency sonar for several weeks prior to birth. When labor seemed imminent, the mother was placed in a custom-designed Plexiglas hot tub that was about 8 feet long on each side. The tub was filled with clear, warm, filtered fresh water. The Plexiglas construction kept the mother separated from the dolphins and yet allowed them to remain close by, enabling the human mother and infant to continue to benefit from exposure to sonar. The babies entered the world in a highly aware, relaxed, blissful state, and later showed signs of a high degree of extrasensory development. John believes that the most beneficial aspect of the dolphins' involvement was the effect of their sonar on the fetus, rather than their presence during the birth.

The Israeli government discouraged the project, and, eventually, the birthing activities were shut down. In reminiscing with me about the project and about the philosophy and goals underlying dolphin-assisted birthing 10 years after it ended, John told me,

> I believe the world was ready then for this new type of birth and human being, and that the world continues to be ready. However, at the time of the Israeli birthing project, the status quo couldn't quite make the shift. Our mission in Israel was to create an ideal, gentle, birthing experience for mother and child, even if that experience stretched existing belief systems. We still hold that vision of birthing fully conscious, highly developed souls into being — souls who will be capable of transforming our world into a place of peace. We believe that a peaceful birth is the blueprint for a peaceful life, and a peaceful life is the blueprint for a peaceful society.

Dolphin-assisted birthing is still practiced in New Zealand, under the guidance of a woman named Estelle Myers. Myers, too, believes that children born through such progressive birthing practices will eventually help to create a new, peaceful generation of human beings on this planet.

Australian dolphin therapy researcher Olivia DeBergerac reports that many Australian hospitals provide water-birthing facilities. "It has been shown that water babies are far less fearful and argumentative. In short, they show the characteristics of human dolphins," she said.[3]

In the 1970s, a small group of men and women explored the possibilities of dolphin-assisted conception. They shared the vision of creating a facility in the South Pacific where a man and woman could go when they wanted to conceive a child. Following a premise similar to that of the Israeli birthing project, the nine months between conception and birth were to be spent in proximity to wild dolphins in uncontrolled, interactive situations. The objective would be to allow the fetus to develop in the dolphins' sonic field, in order to foster the development of a different kind of human.

One of the couples in the group succeeded in conceiving a child in this manner, aided by an ancient Tibetan tantric scripture on consciousness conception. The mother and father anticipated being personally transformed as part of the birthing process. In October 1976, 10 days before the birth, the father, Peter Shenstone, had a powerful psychic experience. While meditating, he began to channel an epic saga that revealed esoteric aspects of the human-dolphin connection. The epic was revealed in a form of compulsive writing known as *automatic writing,* sometimes called *guided writing.* The writing didn't cease until the child's birth. The story that emerged is an oral tradition known today as the legend of the Golden Dolphin.

The legend describes the dolphins' journey from another galaxy to inhabit a small planet that circles Sirius B, and the envoys they later sent to Earth. Consistent with the Dogon legends documented in Richard Temple's scholarly work *The Sirius Mystery,* the legend of the Golden Dolphin reveals the planet in the Sirius star system to be almost entirely aquatic except for two land masses, one of which is home to a small humanoid population. The rest of the planet's inhabitants are cetaceans. One of the humanoid inhabitants is said to have traveled to Earth and made contact with the descendents of the Sirian dolphins who had arrived ahead of him, to have received their blessings, and then to have gone onto the land to create our present human species.

The legend sets forth the relationship between humans and dolphins as being one of sister races, and describes how intergalactic dolphins await us on the other side of our initiation into the "star families."

The Dogon, a North African tribe, actually do have an extensive oral tradition about the Sirius star system. The legend of the Golden Dolphin corroborates aspects of the Dogon mythology concerning the coming of the Nommo, a dolphinlike species. In Dogon mythology, the Nommo arrived on Earth millennia ago in the region of North Africa. But in my reading of *The Sirius Mystery,* I found nothing in the Dogon tradition as it is documented by Temple that substantiates the claim that the dolphin species inhabiting our planet's seas are, indeed, descendents of the Nommo.

For me, the significance of the legend of the Golden Dolphin is its role in reiterating a vital ecological mandate for our planet — the necessity of a rebirth of the human spirit through a reawakening of humankind's innate understanding of how to live in harmony with the living system of the planet. This underlying lesson of the legend is identical to the primal teachings that in native American tradition are called *original instructions.* The traditional wisdom of certain indigenous peoples teaches that the Creator gave humankind these special instructions because, although in many ways we are the weakest of all the beings in Creation, we possess a unique power — the power to upset Earth's natural balance. So, we humans were given ceremonies and lesson stories as remembrances of our proper place in the natural order of things, as native American Joseph Bruchac related:

> Those [original instructions], to put them as simply as possible, were to be kind to each other and to respect the Earth. It is because we human beings tend to forget those instructions that the Creator . . . sends teachers . . . to help us remember and return to the path of the Good Mind. . . . When we follow our Original Instructions, we are equal to the smallest insects and the greatest whales . . . .[4]

The myth of the Nommo as teachers of principles for living in harmony with the Earth also is consistent with concepts put forth by certain well-regarded scientists. The cultural anthropologist Gregory Bateson devoted much of his scholarly consideration to the large units that make up the planet — "not redwoods, but redwood forests; not dolphins, but pieces of oceans."[5]

Bateson's study of dolphins is particularly interesting because he was not observing them in the way a biologist would. His training gave him a different perspective, and as a result he was able to take a fresh view of dolphin behavior and language possibilities. In the course of his observations of dolphin communities, he began to suspect that in place of language, the dolphins have relationships "not only to other dolphins but to oceans, to geography, to navigation, to whatever they deal with."

Bateson asked,

> If it be so that human language with its identification of things and the identification of purposes and all the rest of it leads to an epistemology in which the sensible thing is to eat the environment — and eat up the environment —

> then how do the dolphins [without language, and without an identification of things and purposes] structure their universe?[6]

The answer to Bateson's question may help point the way to the path humans must take if we are to restore balance on the Earth. Viewed alongside scholarly studies of Dogon traditions, his conclusions about dolphins and relationships help to establish a foundation in Western science that corroborates aspects of the legend of the Golden Dolphin.

In addition to an influential role in the evolution of humanity, *Homo delphinus* also offers the possibility of romance and love. In South America, the nearly blind boto, an endangered river dolphin, still makes its home in some rivers. Local legend holds that the boto can shapeshift into a handsome man in order to make a nocturnal foray into a nearby village, where he will choose a village woman to be his lover. Similar occurrences have been reported in places far removed from the Amazon. Photographer Daniel McCulloch, who sometimes facilitates dolphin encounter groups, tells a story about a lucid dream featuring a dolphin-man who emerged from the ocean during a swim charter. The adventure was centered around a participant in his group, a woman in her fifties who had not had a relationship with a man in many years. At the time, this woman's fondest dream was to find a romantic relationship and in that way acquire a ready-made family.

One morning after their charter boat had been among the dolphin pods of the Little Bahama Bank for several days, the woman emerged from her cabin aglow. Encountering Daniel on the deck, she confided to him the reason for her rapturous state. She been visited in her cabin by a dolphin who had then transformed itself into a handsome man. A passionate liaison had followed.

Two days after she recounted her dream, Daniel came onto the deck at dawn and was surprised to find her already in the water, swimming with a dolphin. He inquired whether it might be the same dolphin who had visited her cabin two nights earlier. She said she thought it was.

Months later, the woman told the rest of the story. Not long after returning home, she had met a man who had several children. The two of them fell in love. She believes that the dream experience with her shape-shifting dolphin lover set the stage for the transformation of her life.

Scholars of literature would consider *Homo delphinus* to be an example of hybridity, a common mythological theme. Throughout the progression of literature, many accounts can be found of half-human, half-animal creatures. Now, such themes are reemerging as in modern literature as xenotransplantation, cloning, and other developments in biomedicine rekindle fears of hybridity in the collective human consciousness. Yet, if the ancient fear of hybridity is what dolphin-human represents, *Homo delphinus* offers a twist that is consistent with the seemingly transcendent nature of the dolphin, because when hybridity is applied to the dolphin, the old fear is transformed into a bright hope for the future — a new, more evolved human.

Those who are interested in the evolution of consciousness are already suggesting that humankind needs to develop a meaningful model for what our own species can become at the next stage of its history in order to not be carried forward blindly in the wake of evolution. Even if the dolphins' influence falls short of producing *Homo delphinus,* it still could have far-reaching effects. When human potential movement researcher Peter Russell *(The Global Brain Awakens)* wrote of the quantum leap in consciousness that could mark humankind's next evolutionary advancement, he suggested that the lesser peaks may add up to the greater whole that is is being called for. If this is true, dolphins could influence the course of human evolution by facilitating in us experiences of peak states that bring us closer to the threshold of cosmically expanded awareness.

7

To Swim Or Not To Swim?

[The dolphin's] affection for man renders it dear to the gods,
for it is the only creature who loves man for his
own sake. . . . Though it has no need at all for any man,
yet it is a genial friend to all and has helped many.

Plutarch

It is best for the dolphins' health and welfare to observe them
at a respectful distance, to resist feeding them, and to avoid any
activities that risk harassment such as chasing,
touching or swimming with them.

U.S. Department of Commerce press release

As an introduction to one of his early experimental reports, human-dolphin communication researcher Louis Herman provided the following imaginary conversation between two dolphins:

First dolphin:	"I saw a human swimming!"
Second dolphin:	"Did he leap out of the water? Did his speed reach 14 or more knots? Did he hold his breath for five or more minutes? Did he dive to 300 ft or more? Did he have hard-wired tail flukes?"
First dolphin:	"No, no, no, to all of that."
Second dolphin:	"Well, then, you shouldn't call it swimming. Nothing about it even remotely resembles swimming."[1]

Despite the limitations of the human body, some people have had the thrilling experiencing of swimming with wild dolphins in a manner that comes reasonably close to satisfying the dolphins' criteria for swimming. Patricia Weyer is among the relatively few people who have swum — really *swum* — with wild dolphins. Patricia spends part of each year in wild dolphin habitats and her swimming skills are strong. She described to me how her opportunities for swimming with the pods occurred in stages. First, there was the dolphins' reaction as she cavorted in the water with them: *Hey, you're interesting.* Next, a pod invited her to join them. Patricia did, and soon was heading toward the horizon. She said,

> We swam in formation for about an hour. Along the way, I had several play sessions with the baby dolphin, which slowed the group down. Finally, the adults signaled an end to the play. I did not want to withdraw even though I was exhausted, and, at first, I did not recognize the pods' cue to disengage. But the baby dolphin was their first priority, and the rare privilege I was given had to come to an end. I almost had to be shocked back into my body before I could realize that I would not be able to continue any longer in the encounter.

Saying good-bye to the pod was difficult. I could sense their response: *You're nice but you're not a dolphin, so, be safe. Go back to the boat.*

Swimming back alone, I felt afraid. But I also felt relieved to be released from a situation that neither I nor the dolphins could sustain. Back on board the boat, I lay down on the deck and curled up for a nap. I did not move again for several hours.

On another occasion when she swam with a different pod, she was given a position between a mother and its calf, a placement a prudent dolphin behaviorist would advise against accepting. She hesitated, but the dolphins were adamant, and they won out. As had occurred on the earlier swim, when she was in place, the dolphins set off on a course that headed away from the boat. When she finally stopped to get her bearings, her boat was a dot near the horizon. Sensing that their guest was reaching her limits, two dolphins took positions in front and below her and escorted her most of the way back to the boat.

Human-dolphin dynamics have the most conflicting interpretations of all interspecies relationships. In the myths surrounding cetaceans, the dolphins are variously cast as friends, benefactors, and even teachers of humankind. But now, wild dolphins are being portrayed as our potential enemies by the media. A few years ago, *The New York Times* published an article about dolphins that had the eye-catching title "Evidence Puts Dolphins in a New Light, as Killers." The text of the article described the dolphins as the "killers of the sea." It recounted, in language that was gory and sensational, examples of the carnage that dolphins are known to inflict on each other, including infanticide. *The New York Times'* reporter said the concept of dolphins enjoying the company of humans is dangerously deceptive and noted that wild dolphins often bite, bump, and prod people who attempt to swim with them. The implications for the relationship between dolphins and humanity were dark.

Stories that present a negative viewpoint of human-dolphin interactions appear regularly in syndicated publications around the United States. The anti-dolphin interaction coverage is part of a public relations' campaign against swimming with dolphins. The information sources quoted in these articles are usually National Marine Fisheries Service biologists, who are working for the U.S. Department of Commerce. About a year before *The New York Times'* article appeared I had a telephone conversation with one of the agency's spokespeople. During that conversation, I was informed in a courteous manner that the National Marine Fisheries Service intends to put an end to swim-with-wild-dolphin programs. The spokesperson followed up on our conversation by mailing a press kit to me. The information package was filled with newspaper clippings that discouraged interactions with dolphins, especially the practice of feeding them from boats.

The goal of shutting down wild dolphin swims is supported by the Humane Society of the United States (which for the sake of brevity I refer to hereafter as the Humane Society). The Humane Society has its own related agenda of putting an end to dolphins in captivity. Conservationists in general dismiss the value of "dolphin fondling" programs, objecting that such activities deprive highly intelligent animals of their freedom and put them at risk of disease or mishandling for the sake of public entertainment and commercial gain.

At about the same time I spoke with the National Marine Fisheries Service biologist, I also had an in-person interview with a highly placed representative of the Humane Society, who during our meeting expressed to me not only general disapproval of interactions between the public and dolphins but also a complete lack of interest in interspecies communication.

The concerns held by both of these organizations are valid. But the viewpoint presented in the media coverage they generate is not always complete, and it is based upon a philosophy that considers the perspective of only one faction of our culture — those who still adhere to the traditional scientific paradigm of separatism between human and animal. These people believe that dolphins are to be studied from the approach of the biological and behavioral sciences, which emphasizes numbers, not interspecies communion and friendship. In another era, it was the duty of biologists first to observe animals in their natural habitat and then to collect them as specimens. The latter was called "taking" them, which often was a euphemism for killing the animal. The Marine Mammal Protection Act, passed in 1972 to provide a legal basis for protecting all marine mammals including dolphins and whales, allows for licensed takes of various kinds. Legally killing a dolphin for scientific purposes that fall within the parameters of the Act is termed a *lethal take.* Lethal takes are sanctioned for approved scientific purposes if a permit has been granted. The government defines what constitutes legitimate science.

At the time the Act was passed, swimming with dolphins was not a well-known activity, and so it was not addressed specifically by the law. Today, with swimming encounters becoming increasingly popular, lawmakers are revisiting the ways in which the Act might be updated to counteract current trends. The first step was to issue guidelines on a regional basis. But there is more to come soon. The National Marine Fisheries Service is recommending that swimming with marine mammals of all kinds, not just dolphins, be defined as a "take" by law.

Under this new definition, a permit will be required to swim with wild dolphins and whales. After considering the matter for years, the Fisheries Service made its long-anticipated move at the beginning of 2002 by proposing a rule designed to effectively prevent what it termed "harassment from human activities directed at marine mammals in the wild."[2] Although the National Marine Fisheries Service will not give a timetable, I anticipate that this regulation probably will become law by 2004.

The arguments against swimming with wild dolphins in U.S. coastal waters have focused on two issues. First, the possibility exists that dolphins may be struck by boats, fed tainted fish, shot, or otherwise harassed by nonswimmers. These concerns are particularly valid in the Southeast United States, where hand-feeding fish to dolphins is a popular highlight of marine ecotours. For years, the U.S. government has been moving toward making it illegal for the public to travel by boat to a dolphin habitat for the purpose of interacting with dolphins. In areas like Southeast Florida and Hawaii, where the National Marine Fisheries Service is focusing its enforcement activities, citizen coalitions have formed in an attempt to defuse the situation through self-enforcement, but the government has not responded favorably.

The second common argument against swimming with dolphins concerns the possibility that interaction with humans may be changing the behavior of dolphin pods in a way that will alter the course of their evolution. Whether this concern is actually justified is still arguable. Such interspecies effects are an unavoidable fact of life globally on a planet where the impact of civilization is felt both on land and in the ocean. With myriad activities of humanity and effects of industrialization impacting every part of our world, we cannot avoid affecting the multitude of cultures and species that inhabit the planet.

Others discredit wild swim-with programs by arguing that our human encroachment is stealing something important from wild creatures and, in the process, changing the very nature of the concept of wildness. But the concept of wildness is itself being called into question by some scientists. Does wildness exist, even in the natural state? Cetologist Roger Payne believes that the concept of wildness is our own creation, and that the rest of life on our planet is waiting to accept humans in friendship and peace.[3] Even if this is the case, the question that those of us who swim with dolphins should be asking is whether we are exploiting the dolphin pods when we swim with them. I believe that if we make it our priority to approach them respectfully (a judgment call based on knowledge of dolphin behavior and habits) and to not intrude when our presence is not appropriate (a matter of exercising a little self-restraint), we will not be exploiting them. Instead, we will be fostering interspecies friendship, and both species will reap positive dividends from the encounters.

For the person who wishes to swim with wild dolphins, not exploiting the dolphins calls for thoughtful selection of the swim facilitator. The swim facilitator should be someone who understands dolphin behavior and the species' natural history, and is attuned to the pods' needs. Likewise, the boat captain should be chosen with care, on the basis of his or her reputation as someone who is respectful of the dolphins and does not keep the boat "on a pod" too long during a swim. Since the choice of boat captain is the responsibility of the swim facilitator, selection of a conscientious swim facilitator usually will ensure a conscientious captain and boat crew.

Dolphin experts say that in areas such as certain Hawaiian bays, wild dolphin societies are being disrupted by a plethora of well-intentioned humans seeking a dolphin encounter, but again, their claims are arguable. The fears for wild populations concern the possibility that we are changing the animals' natural behavior in ways that put them at increased risk of injury or death. Attempts at contact may disturb populations by disrupting resting and foraging rhythms, yet biologists do not know whether swim-with activities are actually having this effect.

Not all of our leading cetacean experts hold the same opinions about the solution to the problem. Again, Roger Payne has expressed a view that is strikingly different than the widely held view of wildlife biologists — a view of a future which fosters interspecies interaction and laws that are conducive to interspecies friendships.[4] What impact would shutting down dolphin swimming have for the continued development of our relationship to these beings? Payne is concerned that in becoming overzealous to protect dolphin and whales from harassment, we may stifle important interspecies friendships and fail to maintain or cultivate vital favorable public sentiment on their behalf. I, too, believe the cultivation of favorable public sentiment is best achieved through personal relationships with dolphins. The promotion of a sense of personal connection with the dolphins is, in fact, one of my foremost motivations for leading wild dolphin swims. Most of the people who participate in my groups return home wanting to become advocates for the dolphins, and the dolphins need every advocate they can get, considering the extremely adverse conditions that are developing in the oceans.

Significant progress toward the real solution to the first set of concerns I have described — swimmers' and boaters' encroachment on the dolphins — can be achieved through advocacy and education. The advocates on behalf of dolphins are drawn largely from that part of our population that has had some direct experience with them. To generalize the problems caused by very specific actions, such as feeding or incidents of harassment in particular areas to all locations and the vast majority of swimmers is not fair to either dolphins or people.

The spokespeople whom I have mentioned care deeply about the species they are seeking to protect. The issues underlying the dolphin-swim controversy really are broader and go much deeper into our culture than mere opinions regarding how to safeguard the welfare of the animals, which no one who cares about dolphins would argue against. The real differences of opinion are, I believe, caused by a collision between paradigms. Those two paradigms are symbolized by the characteristics of the left brain and the right brain, or, to put it another way, the masculine and the feminine energies of humanity and Western culture.

The left-brain viewpoint is championed by those who are seeking to ban wild dolphin swim programs. Opposing it is the creative, subjective, and emotionally charged right-brain approach. The chasm between these two world-views is graphically illustrated by the radically different interpretations each faction gives to the streams of bubbles that dolphins sometimes release from their blowholes. Biologists interpret bubbles as a threat or aggressive behavior, or as play-practice for real threats, while some people involved in healing practices interpret the bubbles as containing a communication of expansive energy. If the bubbles contact the human body and especially if they hit the chest, they will help the heart to open, many mystics and healers claim.

Another example of the dual interpretations: In the eyes of biologists, the elaborate spiral bubble formations that the dolphins sometimes blow are intended to entrap and confuse fish. The mystics interpret these figure-eight creations to be intentional representations of the double-helix DNA molecule. They say that these bubble constructions are the dolphins' attempts at reminding us, in the universal language of symbology, that all of Creation shares a common origin.

The interpretation you support will be the interpretation your culture and training has predisposed you to recognize and favor.

The issues surrounding the captive swims are different than the concerns about the wild swims. With captive swims, the biologists representing the National Marine Fisheries Service and the Humane Society of the United States focus on the dozens of injuries sustained by swimmers in the course of swims with captive dolphins — injuries ranging from lacerations to broken bones and shock. The dolphins' aggressive behavior is attributed to the animals' stress level, which is considerable in captivity. But even regarding a seemingly stress-induced event like an injury from a captive dolphin, there may arise a difference of opinion with regard to the dolphin's motivation.

In one often-quoted example, a woman who was rammed by a captive dolphin was taken to the hospital for treatment. Her ribs seemed to be broken, but when she was examined, the x-ray revealed a tumor below the ribs that had not previously been known to exist. The interpretation given by the mystics is that the dolphin rammed the woman to alert her to her medical condition. All the same, she became a number in the statistics that the National Marine Fisheries Service and Humane Society cite to discourage people from swimming with dolphins.

One counter-argument sometimes raised as justification for keeping animals captive is that dolphins do not have the mental faculty to experience boredom in confinement. The animal activists argue against this position. Dolphin activists send out global alerts on the Internet to document horrendous situations in other countries. In some instances the animals are dropped repeatedly during transfer. Those who survive are held captive in inadequate and often inhumane facilities where confinement, lack of shade, chlorination, and water that is too warm or too cold add to discomfort in the new, unnatural environment. All of this leads to suffering and, ultimately, to the tragic death of one or more of the captive dolphins.

The possible conflicts of interest that may arise between captive dolphins and the humans who benefit from them through direct or indirect experiences is a subject that, like possible exploitation in the wild, requires careful thought and appropriate action. We who live in a country like the United States where dolphin captivity is legal need to carefully weigh the benefits that we gain against the adverse effects captivity has on the animals. "Edutainment" of the type provided by theme parks has been shown to have little genuine value in educating the public about marine mammals.

Many of the people who work with captive dolphins develop mixed feelings about the situation. Some eventually take the extreme position. Betsy Smith, the social scientist who developed dolphin-assisted therapy in the 1970s, stopped working with captive dolphins for ethical reasons. After quitting his career as dolphin trainer, Ric O'Barry devoted himself to liberating captive dolphins. Yet, field researcher Roger Payne reminisces about the first whale he saw in captivity when he was a child. He also takes a liberal attitude toward swimming with wild dolphins, because swimming is part of the ecotourism that engenders advocacy for the cetaceans. Having seen a whale or dolphin a few times in the wild, tourists or swimmers will remember the experience for the rest of their lives. Payne believes that through ecotourism, we can learn firsthand what humanity stands to gain by changing its attitude toward the wild world — an unprecedented "Age of Friendship" with the animal kingdom.

No caring person could object to the Department of Commerce's intention to bring an end to irresponsible actions directed at marine mammals. The proposed rule identifies a variety of eco-activities and sporting pastimes, including

> . . . operators of motorized vessels driving through groups of dolphins in order to elicit bow-riding behavior . . . people using underwater "scooters" to closely approach, pursue and interact with the animals . . . [and] operators of personal watercraft tightly circling or crossing through groups of dolphins, often at high speed, to closely approach, pursue and interact with the animals . . . [5]

I have singled out the actions listed in the proposed regulation that seem clearly irresponsible. Other activities named, such as "kayakers and canoers utilizing the quiet nature of their vessels to closely approach and observe or photograph cetaceans . . . [and] whale watchers attempting to touch and pet gray whales . . . " do not outrage me, and I do not believe most biologists would take issue with them. I have seen a photograph of an aged native American woman leaning over the gunwale of a boat to stroke a gray whale while the biologist escorting her stood at the elder's side, smiling. Then, too, there is Roger Payne's charming story in *Among Whales* about a gray whale who, unsolicited, persisted in approaching a small boat and rolling onto his back as an invitation to the skipper to rub his belly.

With regard to the more benign activities such as an unaided but intentional swim-with, and other arguable dolphin-related issues such as whether captive facilities should operate in the United States, I take a position that the government would consider radical. I believe that the dolphins themselves should make the determination. If the dolphins are as intelligent as folk wisdom suggests, they are capable of making their own decisions. Our concern may, therefore, best be placed in doing our part to bridge the communications gap that currently keeps us separated from the dolphins. (Perhaps the government could produce its current version of the long-lost transphonometer, described in Chapter 2, for a practical application that serves the dolphins.) We must learn to communicate with them not just for our own human-centered purposes, but also so that we can achieve a true meeting of the minds. In the process, they will reveal their own desires, preferences, and culture to us.

8

The Surrogate Dolphin

You lie down on the table and wait while an attendant adjusts the stereo-optic display and attaches the neurophone electrodes. The bed begins to gently undulate as a 3-D underwater scene fills your vision. As you try to orient yourself to the direction of this strange and wonderful sound, a dolphin darts by you, giving you a comforting glance with his soulful eye. The experience continues as you playfully encounter each of the six dolphins and join their pod in a high-speed race around a beautiful reef.

The AquaThought Foundation

If the conditions that make a dolphin encounter beneficial for many people can be effectively isolated and analyzed, they might be effectively simulated, as some technologists and scientists are now seeking to do. Virtual reality or a similar approach may allow people to experience aspects of the dolphin essence without risk of impacting dolphin populations, and also may revolutionize the way the public encounters dolphins.

Researcher Horace Dobbs first observed the mood-elevating effects that dolphins have on clinically depressed people in 1974. In 1986, he launched a project that aimed to provide people who are suffering from clinical depression with an alternative to anti-depression medications. His program, Operation Sunflower, combined music and dolphin sounds, accompanied by auto-suggestion methods, on audio cassette. In the process, Dobbs realized that dolphin images induce psychological neurological recovery, which is explained by a new branch of medicine, psycho-neurological immunity. His experiments with dolphin images and music for therapeutic purposes continued. Eventually, he developed a dolphin therapy pool, which featured dolphin images in the form of holograms combined with the soothing effects of water and dolphin sounds.

In the mid-1990s, dolphin imagery took the inevitable leap into virtual reality with the AquaThought Foundation's announcement of CyberFin, a simulation designed to realistically reproduce, through three-dimensional images, vibration, and audible sound, the sensory experience that accompanies human-dolphin interactions. AquaThought incorporated a neurophone and a hydrophone into the device, which has a liquid-crystal mattress that simulates the sensation of floating in water.

In enthusiastic reviews at the product's launch, the media declared that CyberFin fills "a gap left by the virtual reality industry that mostly offers competitive, shoot-em-up adventures." *Wired Magazine*'s Judy Bryan said the AquaThought Foundation had developed "an elegant way of bringing the dolphin swim experience to people everywhere. . . . the first VR that's as comfortable as it is enticing."[1]

CyberFin's developers envisioned their invention's role in fostering "a greater understanding of our intelligent neighbors on the planet and an awakening interest in making contact."[2] Their goal was to bring dolphins to a mass audience by virtually transporting users of all ages into a marine world populated with friendly dolphins.

The neurophone reproduced the massive acoustic energy that is sometimes perceived underwater during an interaction with an echolocating dolphin.[3] "Guests should be prepared for an intense sensory experience," AquaThought's Web site advised. A monthly lease was priced at about $900. To ensure a niche for their product, the company's research team simultaneously attempted to provide scientific proof of the benefits of dolphin interaction.

Envisioning an important market niche in therapy, the AquaThought Foundation installed CyberFin at Loma Linda University Medical Center in California to help calm children following surgery. Another unit was put into operation at the New Jersey State Aquarium in Camden, and the public was invited to take a virtual frolic with the dolphins.

Devices like CyberFin seem to offer a reasonable solution to the biological and ethical arguments that some people are raising against swimming with wild and captive dolphins. But, as the aquarium staff discovered, the installation did not meet up to expectations. In retrospect, the aquarium's management concedes that the shortfall may have been due, in part, to limitations in the way the facility presented CyberFin. The aquarium was not large enough for a separate space to be set aside to house the installation, nor could an attendant be allocated for its operation. Also, many visitors balked at paying an additional five dollars for a virtual foray into the marine world. After about a year and a half, the New Jersey State Aquarium returned the CyberFin unit to AquaThought.

While CyberFin was on the premises, staff member Brian DuVall went for a virtual snorkel with the dolphins. "There were some perceptual issues," he recalls. "Lying on your back on the table, you were supposed to imagine that you were snorkeling. But you weren't face down, and you felt the dolphins' sounds and vibrations on the wrong side of the body. So, the user couldn't integrate sensory input in a normal way."

Whatever CyberFin's fate as a product, technologists undoubtedly will continue to experiment with new applications for neurotechnology in dolphin-related research, providing new answers to the question *Why dolphins?*

As exciting and convincing to the senses as technologists may one day be able to make such devices, something important will always be missing in the virtual world. In the real world, both dolphins and the sea represent an edge — a novel experience that challenges existing belief systems and perceptions. Like all marginal areas, edges create anxiety, but they also stimulate us to redefine reality and to expand in novel directions. To explore an edge is to confront uncertainties and dangers as part of a passage into a new relationship with oneself as well as a new relationship between oneself and the external world.

It is not only the dolphins who represent an edge, it is also the ocean. Some of the people who have participated in my ocean swims have spoken of their fears related to entering the water, usually as the result of near-drowning experiences that occurred much earlier in their lives. For each of these people, swimming with dolphins was a way of confronting a deeply held fear. At the end of the encounter week, one woman told me how, seeing two dolphins near her in the water, she was suddenly reminded of the two young men who had rescued her from the sea many years earlier. As a result, she was able to put to rest her long-standing anxieties about being in the ocean.[4]

Historically, our culture's interspecies' edges have involved conquest. Bull-fighting and whaling are two examples. But today, as new dynamics emerge in our culture and we increasingly acknowledge and honor feminine energy, the desire for communion is replacing the goal of conquest. This desire for communion has much to do with why swimming with dolphins is becoming popular.

The matter of *conquest* versus *communion* came to my attention as the result of two separate discussions. In the first, as I was describing the results of my peak research to someone, he began to nod in recognition. It was, he said, the kind of experience his hunter friends described. As an advocate for the animals and compassionate human-animal interactions, I was appalled by his comment. He was speaking of conquest, not communion. At the time, however, I could think of no reply other than that the thrill of hunting wasn't the kind of peak experience I had been considering.

At about that same time, several anonymous scholars were reading one of my journal submissions in the traditional prepublication screening process known as *peer review.* One of the reviewers suggested a possible connection between the dolphin-triggered peak and the element of fear that emerges in high-risk, high-thrill activities such as parachute diving or white-water rafting. I did not feel that fear was a significant element in the process I was describing — quite the opposite, in fact — and submitted a counter argument. I must have been sufficiently convincing, because the article was approved for publication. But my reviewer had a point. In his book *Dolphins,* journalist Tim Cahill described his own experience of swimming with a pod of dolphins, and the high-thrill aspect is evident:

> You're in the water now, looking in all directions, but there's nothing there, just clear water fading off into a distance of blue and green, the color of the sky before a tornado. And then here they come! Several waterborne creatures swimming toward you, moving fast. They're bigger and faster than you expected. One shoots directly by your side. . . . *Whoa. Is this guy coming at me broadside, is he going*

> *to head-butt?* No, its head is turned a bit, and the whole body curves away from you as it sweeps past. . . . and in that couple of seconds, your emotion has gone from fear to a kind of strange elation — because this is a big animal, much faster in the water than you ever imagined, and it could kill you if it wanted. But . . . there was something in the dolphin's eye. The creature seemed curious. Intelligent. As if it were inviting you to dance, and to swim as you've only swum in your dreams.[5]

Cahill's experience comes close to bridging the high-thrill risk and elated peak experience aspects. But a piece of the puzzle is missing. In considering the matter, I eventually realized that the three subjects — wild-animal-triggered peak experience, high-thrill sports, and the hunters' high — *are* related, but in an unexpected way. The high-thrill peak, which is based on confronting fear, is closely akin to the thrill of hunting, and both of these experiences, I believe, stand in opposition to the transcendent, *beyond-the-self* experience that the wild-animal-triggered peak encounter encompasses. This realization came upon me after I read a commentary by the world's leading authority on whales, Roger Payne. In his book *Among Whales*, Payne acknowledged the excitement of the stalk, having to overcome fear, the grandeur of the quarry and the hunter's respect for it. But the problem with trophy hunters, he went on to say,

---

> is that although they are brave enough to face and kill their prizes, they are not imaginative enough to risk a sustained relationship with them, except when they are dead and all possible danger in such relationships is laid to rest. . . . [The real challenge lies] in learning how to live with your quarry — learning how to extract the same thrill, without in the end straddling its dead body — without dominating it utterly and claiming ownership of it. . . . The challenge before us is to confederate with nature in new ways . . . In this way, we will also heal ourselves.[6]

The key is the ability to let go of control and the desire to dominate, and, in so doing, open up to experiencing a wild-animal encounter based on friendship and joyful, spontaneous communion. As play expert Fred Donaldson has said, "Suppose that instead of engaging animals with a 30/30 we learned to touch them with our hands."[7] That moment of experiencing provides opportunity for personal and societal transformation while also serving as the key to healing interspecies' relationships.

9

"The Whales And Porpoises Know"

The dolphins are beaching themselves. They are creating diseases
within themselves. This is their way of refusing to continue to live
upon the Earth. They feel that they cannot fulfill the purpose
for which they are born. Therefore, they are leaving. . . .
The dolphin manifests itself — dolphins are born — to bring
love and life and creativity to the oceans. They manifest to form
a bridge of joy and love and intelligence between the
aquatic kingdom and the human kingdom.
This they cannot do.

Gary Zukav

Swimming with dolphins is not the only way we are impacting dolphin populations long-term, and, in fact, consideration of the other influences puts the relatively marginal effects of dolphin swims in a more realistic perspective. One of the greatest threats facing life in the ocean today is the active sonar technologies that navies of the world are developing for deployment. Several variations on this surveillance sonar exist, and each is potentially lethal to marine life under certain circumstances. The technology that I have heard the most about and that has touched closest to my own life is Surveillance Towed Array Sensor System Low Frequency Active (SURTASS LFA) Sonar.

In spring of 2000, whale biologist Ken Balcomb serendipitously witnessed and was able to study a mass stranding of whales and one dolphin that was caused by a sonar exercise in the Bahamas. In an open letter to the U.S. Navy, Balcomb stated that the incident unequivocally demonstrated the lethality of high-powered sonars, and provided the opportunity to understand how sonar was inadvertently killing whales in vast expanses of ocean around the world.

Such deaths, he said, are largely due to resonance phenomena in cetaceans' cranial air spaces. Delicate tissues are torn apart around the brain and ears. Prior to March 2000, the struggle between the Navy and the cetacean advocates had focused on auditory thresholds and traumas in sea mammals, which also constitute an important argument against the deployment of the sonar. But Balcomb's timely discovery of the whale and dolphin carcasses on the beach near his seasonal home in the Bahamas enabled him to obtain fresh tissue samples from the dead animals. For the first time, it was possible to prove the cause of death.

In an open letter to the SURTASS LFA program manager, Balcomb stated, "now I have seen the problem and can attest to the fact that there is massive injury to whales caused by sonar. This is not an exaggerated statement . . . "[1] Through his technical and scientific knowledge, Balcomb was able to show that the Navy already possessed sufficient information to know theoretically of the lethal consequences that even brief exposure to the towed sonar would have on marine mammals — knowledge that was being publicly denied.

Balcomb pointed out to the Naval program manager that resonance can dramatically contribute to extremely damaging shear forces that are capable of tearing wings off airplanes and collapsing buildings. In living tissue, vertigo, dizziness, and hemorrhaging occur. When LFAS is activated within range of a marine mammal, a dolphin or whale cannot travel fast enough to escape serious injury. The physical trauma to the animal, Balcomb concluded, "is both astonishing and bloody."

LFAS is scheduled for deployment oceanwide. When I began writing this chapter in the fall of 2001, Congress was holding LFAS hearings in Washington, D.C. A few weeks later, while congressional hearings were still in progress, rumors were circulating on the Internet regarding the U.S. Navy's latest round of sonic testing, off the coast of Japan. In the interim, Congressional testimonies were offered on cetaceans' behalf by expert witnesses who presented impressive evidence that the sonics created by the proposed oceanic surveillance systems are killing whales and dolphins or causing them to become severely disoriented.

Pod displacement, which can result from nonlethal activities like human swimming, is among the dangers of LFAS. One scientific witness who is opposed to the oceanwide deployment of a sonar network pointed out to Congress that displacement of pods to a new location would constitute a significant change in biologically important behavior and could even threaten the pod's continued existence.

LFAS stands to have much more of an effect on dolphin evolution than any amount of swim-with-dolphin activity that might disrupt the patterns of certain populations on a highly localized basis. Compared to the widespread and lethal threats of LFAS, the effects of recreational swimming with dolphins are inconsequential. Swimming with dolphins quickly becomes a nonissue if there will be no more dolphins left in the ocean in a decade or two anyway due to the devastating oceanwide effects of sonar surveillance.

Public outcry on behalf of the dolphins, whales, and other sea creatures is urgently needed to keep biologically destructive technologies like LFAS out of the ocean.

The Navy was testing its LFAS weapon in the humpback nursery area off the coast of the Big Island of Hawaii in 1998 during one of my dolphin swim trips there. At that time, the Navy was still denying that LFAS is known to have any negative effects on marine mammals. Yet, its Web site contained information about the damaging effects of LFA sonar on human tissue, and specified the precautions the military was taking to protect crew members aboard ships equipped with the sonar towing array.

While I was on the Big Island, I had seen advisories posted at several of the more popular swimming areas on the Kona Coast. The government was notifying the public that for a two-month period, swimmers should be on the alert for any unusual symptoms in themselves such as nausea, headaches, earaches, chest pains, dizziness, and disorientation, and should report the occurrence of such symptoms to the Public Health Department or the Navy.

Between my ocean swims off the Kona Coast, I had placed phone calls to the Navy's public relations liaison officer in Honolulu. I was trying to orchestrate time aboard the LFAS ship as a visitor, an opportunity that was being offered to activists and certain others as part of Navy public relations' efforts.

Initially, I was granted approval to board with a group of students from the University of Hawaii, based on my own status as a scientific researcher. I received specific instructions for meeting the inflatable Zodiac that the big ship would be sending into the harbor. But after agreeing to that much, the Navy public relations officer asked me the subject of my research ("not that it matters," he added). When I told him I was interested in peak human experience triggered by encounters with cetaceans, he quickly ended the conversation, claiming he had another call coming in. I was not able to reach him by telephone again after that, even though he had given me his pager number. I went to the dock anyway, at what I understood to be the Zodiac's appointed departure time. No one was there.

A government consultant with whom I discussed the subject of LFAS at length during my flight from Hawaii back to the mainland sincerely believed that the government would not do anything that might have an adverse effect on wildlife. Yet, as Ken Balcomb has since pointed out, the Navy knows that the cetacean auditory system is affected by the ranges in which the LFAS works.

A rumor is circulating among some of the people who swim with dolphins semi-professionally. It concerns a statement allegedly made by a high-ranking naval officer to the effect that within 10 years, there won't *be* any dolphins. Two people have mentioned this statement to me in the last couple years. Neither of my informants knew who the source was, so I do not know whether the remark — if, indeed, it is a genuine off-the-record comment — was made by a single officer or by two officers.

When people learn of my connection with the dolphins, they often have a story to tell. I have collected numerous interesting anecdotes in this way, but none is as unusual as the one shared by a Canadian woman, Gail Prowse. Gail had received an after-death communication concerning the dolphins and whales. People are increasingly speaking out about having received after-death messages from departed loved ones, so after-death communication can no longer be relegated to the domain of seances. Some of the individuals who are reporting these experiences are highly esteemed people who, through their candor, are bringing credibility and respectability to the topic. (For example, in her autobiography *Reason for Hope: A Spiritual Journey*, Jane Goodall described an after-death visitation she received from her husband, who had recently passed away.)

Gail's adventure began one winter day when she went for a drive alone in the mountains of Canada. Although the weather had been pleasant and absolutely clear when Gail set off on her outing, she suddenly found herself engulfed in a swirling snowstorm. When a semitruck careened by, she totally lost control of her auto. The wind and slippery conditions nearly sent her over the edge of a cliff. When the vehicle came to a stop, one tire was hanging over the edge of the precipice. As Gail sat rigid and white-faced behind the wheel, another truck stopped, and the driver walked over to her auto and opened the door. He assured her he would help and told her to sit with his wife in the safety of his vehicle. After Gail's auto was back on the road, the wife insisted that Gail come home with them for the night.

The next morning, when Gail came downstairs for breakfast, her hostess said, "I've had a visitor here with me this morning." She went on to describe Gail's beloved grandfather, who had died on that very date 15 years earlier. As Gail listened in amazement, the wife gave a detailed account of her visitation with the grandfather, of whom the wife had had no prior knowledge. After relaying a brief personal message of love and caring from the old man, who seemed to know recent details of his granddaughter's life, including the fact that she had entered graduate school, the wife said,

---

> He says he is very, very worried about the ocean. "What are we doing to our seas?" He was shaking his head and gesturing with his hands. "Education!" he exclaimed. "What good is education when we are destroying the oceans? The whales and porpoises know — they are calling to you to help. You must do something soon." He went on about this for a long time.

The woman was very puzzled about the message and wondered why it had come to her houseguest. "Are you involved with any kind of whale-saving group?" she asked.

In describing her experience to me, Gail assured me that it was not surprising that her grandfather should carry a message about the seas to her. He had been a sea captain and had sailed all over the world in double-masted schooners and large tankers. He also had been a fisherman. But her own life had nothing to do with the ocean or the whales and dolphins, nor had she ever been a member of any environmental group. She had no idea how to respond to her grandfather's plea. So she passed the call for help on to me.

What are the hazards the grandfather was warning about? I already knew about the dangers dolphin populations face. I have described the situation surrounding the U.S. military's active sonar surveillance system and how it is creating a significant global threat for the dolphins and whales. Unless the concerned citizens, activists, and scientists who oppose the active sonar are able to prevail against the military machine, a global sound network is imminent. Even before the war on terrorism, the mood at the federal level was not in favor of scuttling a military program years in the making at a cost of hundreds of billions of tax dollars. Now, with the free world confronting its worst societal fears and paranoias, who will want to quibble about matters of national security?

Another of the hazards is the pollution of the seas with highly toxic chemicals that are absorbed and retained in the body's fatty tissues, where they compromise the immune system. The effects of the toxins are especially noticeable in those species that are high up on the food chain, because the toxins accumulate as they are passed on in food. Toxic pollution is destroying life in the ocean as it gives seawater the functional equivalent of AIDS. This terrible condition impacts not only all marine mammals, but also many other creatures, aquatic and nonaquatic.

Years before all of this became widely recognized, the author Gary Zukav stated in *The Seat of the Soul* that the dolphins are leaving the planet. A geological chronology of dolphin history shows that dolphins were far more abundant in the oceans back in the Miocene and Pliocene eras than they are now. Extinctions are a reality of the evolutionary process, but this time it is human-created circumstances that are causing dolphins to leave the planet. Zukav said their species' demise is being brought about by an exhaustion of the dolphin soul as the result of the brutality of our own species. If a global deployment of active sonar occurs, not only dolphins but also many other large marine mammals will probably leave the planet, destroyed by the sonar's lethal frequencies.

I am greatly saddened by this probability, but perhaps my reaction is selfish. I am, after all, a mermaid whose fantasy is to return to the sea. If the dolphins and whales leave, and many of the other sea creatures follow them, the sea will become a lonely place for me. Traditional native American belief holds that species that become extinct still exist in the archetypal realms, a possibility that gives me some small comfort. So, I am sometimes able to transmute the ominous forecast of the dolphins' departure into a visual metaphor of transcendence and beauty. My icon for this transformation is an image created by the visionary artist John Pitre. The painting hangs in a gallery in Kailua-Kona on the Big Island, Hawaii. Every time I lead a dolphin encounter group on the Kona Coast, I stop by the gallery to view the painting. The scene it depicts always brings tears to my eyes, but, along with those tears, I also feel filled with a quiet peace. The image shows a tropical ocean filled with dolphins who are ascending from the sea to the sky through a circular rainbow. This symbol of transformation is the vision I hold in my heart for the dolphins.

10

The Question Of Personhood

One of my colleagues . . . who has no interest whatever in animal rights, concedes that he would be greatly interested in these questions if we found an animal that could speak.

Bernard Rollins

Much as I think dolphins are extraordinary creatures, I'm wary of raising them above the rest of the animal kingdom, of saying that dolphins — along with humans, of course — outshine everything else. Thus far, anyway, we have more concrete evidence of the intelligence, language abilities, tool use, culture, and so on for chimps than we do for dolphins. They are certainly much closer to us genetically. Are we to consider them persons, too? Maybe. So where do we draw the line between "personhood" and "nonpersonhood?"

Carol Howard

My position as an advocate for interaction with dolphins takes into consideration the benefits that both dolphin and human stand to realize from such friendships. On the human side, we all know the pitfalls of isolating ourselves culturally — the bigotry, the misunderstandings, the missed opportunities for expanded horizons. Traditional native American cultures view nonhuman animals as peoples in their own right. But *animals as persons* is a concept that has yet to find acceptance in Western cultures. So, I would like to see the U.S. government sanction swimming with wild dolphins — provided, of course, that the swimmers show proper regard for the dolphins — and I would also like to see society become more progressive in championing animals as persons, for the protection the status of personhood affords in the event of human misconduct. I believe it will be through such an enlightened public consciousness, rather than through placement of restrictions on one-on-one relationships with wild species like dolphins and whales, that we will most effectively protect all creatures.

Roger Fouts, a major contributor to the field of interspecies communication (see Chapter 2), is an advocate for the rights of his chimpanzee research subjects and other captive chimpanzees. Fouts believes that the time may now be right to push forward the goal of personhood for nonhuman animals, using the chimpanzee as the fulcrum species, because of the close genetic ties that exist between chimps and humans, and the chimps' demonstrated culture and individuality. But the rationale for extending personhood to animals goes much deeper than even that, as Fouts emphasized when he told me, "We are all related — 50 percent of the genetic code of all life on Earth is the same. Darwin specifically pointed out the arbitrariness of the distinction we draw when we speak of species. The concept of species was created to provide convenient categories, but people treat it as real."[1]

Though lacking the "right" genetics and an easily observable culture, and at risk of being deprived (in the eyes of human society) of individuality by laws aimed at keeping them remote from most of the human population, dolphins are another of the prime candidate species for personhood.

The keenness of dolphin intelligence may still be arguable, but we humans are becoming increasingly open to acknowledging other kinds of intelligence as no less important than those attributes such as IQ which we have traditionally favored for their human-centeredness. Dolphins possess a charisma that is generated in part by that intelligence, and also by their benevolence toward humans, their approachability, their spontaneity, and their other admirable qualities. All of these attributes could help cast the dolphin in the role of model species for personhood.

An official attempt was made in that direction in the 1970s, when Sidney Holt, a Fisheries and Environment advisor to the Food and Health Organization of the United Nations, produced a memorandum addressed to members of the Advisory Committee on Marine Resources Research. He exhorted committee members to widen their perspective and concede that intelligence is not confined to humankind. Several decades have passed since Holt's suggestion of a special status for cetaceans. The Marine Mammal Protection Act of 1972 was put in place to keep marine mammals safe from harassment, but cetaceans have not yet achieved recognition as persons.

One of the landmark trials touching on the question of animal personhood involved dolphins. It took place in Hawaiian courts in 1977, and involved a charge by the University of Hawaii against two men who had worked in the laboratory of dolphin communication researcher Louis Herman. Herman's former assistants (one of whom was Kenneth LeVasseur, who had been Dwight Batteau's colleague; see Chapter 2) had broken into his facilities late one night and stolen two valuable experimental dolphins — an act that set back the University's communication research by years, Herman pointed out. The thieves transported the dolphins to a bay and freed them. In court, they claimed that the conditions of captivity had threatened the dolphins' lives, and that their action had been carried out to call attention to unsatisfactory laboratory conditions.

Herman countered that the release of the dolphins, who were unprepared for the rigors of surviving in the wild, almost surely consigned two valuable pieces of state property to death. In ruling against the disgruntled assistants, the judge based his decision on the meaning of the words "other" and "person." The judge did not believe that a dolphin could be considered "another," which in his view clearly meant another person. Dolphins were defined as property in that court of law. In rejecting the assistants' pleas, the judge said he did not know at what level the intelligence of an animal became sufficient for the animal to be treated like a human being under the penal code. In the mind of that judge, dolphins were not equal to humans under the penal code, with a certain undefined level of intelligence being the condition for protection.

Today, most people still consider intelligence to be the primary criterion for personhood. At the same time, the intuitive beliefs that many people hold about dolphins suggest a level of intelligence that is higher than that of most other species, including, in some regards, our own.

Personhood is a societal concept. We consider animals to be individuals, and zoologists use the word *persons* to signify the individual members of a compound or colonial organism. But animals are not considered persons. A bit of background about animal rights is helpful in understanding the context for this position. Prior to 1822, no form of animal cruelty legally existed without an infringement on the rights of ownership. Little has changed. Today, an animal that represents a domesticated species is considered property under law, and the rights that are involved in a court case are the rights of the animal's human "owner," which are defined by legislation. Ironically, an animal gets less consideration under law than an inanimate legal entity like a corporation. For the wild animal, matters are even worse. Wild animals have no legal rights at all, because, lacking an owner, they are basically outside of the law.

Facilities housing wild animals are more humane today than those of earlier times, especially in the United States. We have learned from our own dark era of dolphin captivity, which sometimes involved horrific exhibitions like a display staged in the 1970s by a showman who traveled around the United States transporting a lone dolphin from town to town in a coffinlike container. In each new town, a small temporary pool was set up around the sarcophagus. After the pool was filled with water, the sides of the container were lowered and the dolphin was put on display. When the novelty ceased to draw crowds, the sides of the container were raised, the pool was drained, and the exhibit was transported to the next town. Because keeping a dolphin over the winter would have been costly, the handler killed the dolphin at the end of the season and extracted its teeth for souvenirs. The next spring, he obtained another dolphin and headed out on his circuit again. Over the years, a huge pile of dolphin teeth accumulated.[2]

Such a concession could not operate in the United States today, and many far less injurious captive facilities also have closed. Some other countries are even more progressive. The citizens of the United Kingdom have successfully shut down every captive dolphin facility in their commonwealth. Elsewhere in Europe, other facilities are beginning to follow suit, and the trend is spreading slowly to other parts of the world, thanks to the efforts of determined activists.

Contemporary dolphin researchers in the United States are sensitive to the problems their captive subjects face. Many of them have struggled with the ethics of the situation in the course of finding a way to justify their work. For example, Carol Howard, the author of *Dolphin Chronicles,* decided in the course of her research that for all the problems that captivity creates, it still has value because it affords a basis for understanding through a shared world. But a shortsightedness sometimes seems to exist around our dolphin-related activities both captive and wild, whether they involve communication experiments, healing, or education. We invest considerable time, energy, and resources in our pursuits surrounding dolphins, and we may feel that we love the species. Yet, many people who love dolphins and in some way keep the dolphins in their lives still neglect to actively promote the species' welfare or its personhood.

An animal's degree of self-awareness or intelligence does not make sense as the criterion for personhood, in view of the criteria that we apply within our own species. In 1974, lawyer and economist Christopher Stone pointed out how the problems of legal incompetents (a legal incompetent is a human being who has become "vegetable") are handled: a court of law designates someone to manage the incompetent's affairs. Stone suggested that the legal problems of natural objects be approached in the same way. Under such a system, when a friend of a natural object perceives that object (which could be an animal such as a dolphin) to be endangered, that interested party could apply to a court for the creation of a guardianship.

Stone's brilliant essay, *Should Trees Have Legal Standing? Toward Legal Rights for Natural Objects,* was written five years before the trial of Louis Herman's research assistants. He issued it to coincide with a landmark legal battle that held important implications for personhood. The case, *Sierra Club* vs. *Morton,* was heard by the U.S. Supreme Court. (Morton was a land development company that intended to develop Mineral King, a remote scenic recreational land in California, into a Disneyland.) The case made clear the fact that animals are not "legal persons" in the way that humans, ships, corporations and municipalities are. In the course of the trial, the dissenting justices gave serious discussion to the matter of natural objects being entitled to legal standing, and Stone's paper provided important material for their consideration. Stone's intention was that the paper should become a vehicle for advancing his theory that societies, like human beings, progress through different stages of sensitiveness. He was envisioning that our society might be evolving into a culture in which Nature and natural objects possess legal rights.

The serious consideration given to Christopher Stone's treatment of the issue does seem to suggest that societal viewpoints on animals as persons may change in the future. Stone was calling for a radical new approach to humankind's relationship to Nature. Such a changed consciousness would, he said, not only be a step toward solving our material planetary problems, it would also make far better humans of us. "As radical as such a consciousness may sound today, all the dominant changes we see about us point in its direction," Stone said.[3]

One of the interesting facts underlying *Sierra Club vs. Morton* is that the Sierra Club actually lacked a legal standing for challenging the developers' intention regarding Mineral King, because Sierra Club could not meet the "injury in fact" test. Injury in fact requires more than an injury to a cognizable interest — it requires that the party seeking review be among the injured. Even though members of Sierra Club used the park for recreational purposes, and the development of the land stood to destroy or otherwise impair its scenic quality, Sierra Club could not meet the test.

The legal concepts that apply to Mineral King extend to other aspects of Nature including individual animals. But we are still awaiting the practical innovations. Today, animals domestic and wild, including Roger Fouts's signing chimpanzees and Louis Herman's dolphins, still have no more legal status than inanimate property. Dolphins and whales are "conserved" under the Office of Protected Resources. Dolphin-assisted therapy is regulated by the U.S. Department of Agriculture's Office of Animal and Plant Health Inspection Services. These jurisdictions are revealing of the fact that, far from enjoying the privileges that come with any semblance of personhood, these species continue to be viewed as resources and commodities.

At this point in the evolution of our society, we still seem far from granting personhood to natural objects. But, given the chimpanzees' genetic similarities to *Homo sapiens* and the great apes' aptitude for communicating with us in a language of our own invention, as well as the many charismatic qualities of the dolphins, an intermediate milestone may be achievable. Consideration of personhood for chimpanzees and dolphins may provide impetus for taking the next step in the natural progression of society under the evolutionary scenario described by Stone.

One of my hopes for the accomplishments of humankind within my lifetime is that animals and natural objects will achieve legal standing. I know that there are many truly caring people who would help make this happen if they knew how to contribute. I met two of them while I was camped on a beach in Hawaii. Jean-Pierre and Christina were welcoming opportunities to swim with the dolphin pods that sometimes visit the bay where the campground is located. In our conversations, they described their recent humanitarian mission to Guatemala, and we discussed my reasons for coming to Hawaii to see the dolphins as well as my interest in interspecies communication.

At the end of my stay, Jean-Pierre asked me a question that no one had asked me before: *When all is said and done, what do I hope to have accomplished for the animals?*

I described to him my desire to see animals acquire the legal protections afforded by personhood, and, also, my vision of how dolphins might serve as a bridge to that goal. He nodded and then brought out a portfolio containing photographs of the sculptures and jewelry he has designed. As I admired his work, he offered to design a piece of jewelry for sale through my nonprofit organization, to raise funds for advancing animal rights goals. "I wouldn't normally do something like that, but I would do it for the dolphins," he said.

I know there are many people like Jean-Pierre who would go the extra mile for the dolphins.

In dolphin circles, mention is often made of the dolphins' supposed gifts to humankind. Instead of focusing exclusively on the dolphins' potential gifts to us and to the world, we might do better for the planet if we follow Jean-Pierre's example and consider what gift we can give to the dolphins.

One of those gifts is easily carried out from home and without any special talent. Through participation in Internet listservers (e-mail information groups that send out periodic alerts informing subscribers about a variety of subjects ranging from LFAS to proposed new captive dolphin facilities in emerging nations) dolphin admirers can stay informed about human activities that impact wild and captive dolphins. Friends of the dolphins can write letters to discourage countries from giving permits for proposed captive swim programs, and by boycotting programs that exploit captive dolphins. Tourists in search of dolphins can seek destinations and programs that offer an environment in which marine mammals can be enjoyed in their own habitats and on their own terms.

Friends of all animals can do a great interspecies service by learning more about the existing laws regarding animal protection, and then supporting legislative reform. The cultivation of generous attitudes like those held by humanitarians Jean-Pierre and Christina can help us to achieve an interspecies community of dolphins and humans working together in partnership to benefit all of Creation.

11

Visioning A World Dream

We stand poised on the edge of a new millennium. The future of humankind and of the planet rests in the balance.

Liza Tenzin-Dolma

The most important aspect of my dolphin work is the positive impact it has on people and, ultimately, on the dolphins and whales themselves. When I make a public presentation, I often begin by invoking the presence of the dolphins briefly with a short audio segment of dolphin sounds, and I end with an ecological message on behalf of the creatures of the sea. After one conference presentation, a woman named Alexis McKenna came up to me at the podium and said, "While I was listening to the dolphins, I found myself crying. Why did they affect me that way?" I responded with the first thought that came into my mind: "It's because the dolphins are calling you." That must have been true, because she signed up for one of my wild dolphin swims.

Alexis was the most diligent participant I have yet had in my encounter groups. She engaged me in several e-mail discussions about dolphins before the actual trip, and she read most of the books on my suggested reading list. While we were together with the dolphins in Hawaii, she was usually the first swimmer in the water and the last to climb back onto the boat.

A year later, I contacted her to ask how her experiences surrounding the dolphins seemed to have impacted her life. She replied that she was visioning a dream around them, as a step toward manifesting that dream in the world. "I write at least one world dream each year and then incubate it in my dream journal. I try to focus on it regularly, but don't always get it done. At least it's written down, and I know that matters," she explained.

For the year following her dolphin encounter, her world dream was about the Cetacean Nation, a concept first put forth by John Lilly, the scientist who pioneered dolphin studies. Alexis's desire to incubate such a vision as a world dream demonstrates the power of the dolphins' call. As a vision for the new millennium, her dream is one which all of those who love the dolphins, whales, and humanity will want to share.

John Lilly dreamed that the cetaceans (dolphins and whales) will eventually be recognized as a sentient species. Once that happens, he dreamed, they will be granted official representation and a voice on the governing bodies of planet Earth. (The native Hawaiian people already have a cetacean ambassador.)

I am dreaming of the discovery of a Rosetta Stone that will allow us to crack the code of communication with cetaceans. Specifically, this knowledge will allow us to establish, beyond a shadow of doubt, that cetaceans are sentient beings with their own sound language, and also that cetaceans create social structures and engage in social interactions. As a result of this discovery, cetaceans will be declared protected species. It will no longer be possible for anyone anywhere in the world to slaughter, capture, or enslave cetaceans. They, like native peoples, will be recognized as an indigenous species. They will be granted the right of representation on world governing bodies. Their voices will be raised; their points of view will be heard. Their magnificent healing abilities, too long unrecognized and unused by human beings, will be recognized and acclaimed.

Cetaceans will begin training those human beings who already possess the natural talents and abilities to use sound healing techniques, for the good of our planet and our world. Many diseases previously thought untreatable will respond to their warm, joyous healing sounds. People will experience miraculous healings and personal transformations.

Those people who discover the Rosetta Stone will be protected from harm by God–Goddess–All That Is, and by those other positive invisible forces that want to see humanity evolve into a new state of consciousness. In ways magical and mysterious, the keys to breaking the sound code of cetacean language will be safely brought forth and shared with all humanity. Perhaps there will be a simultaneous release of the information all over the world as there was with the mapping of the human genome.

Here's the point: This knowledge will be freely available to all. It will not be suppressed. Even though this knowledge will create an enormous psychological burden of guilt and shame for humanity, that guilt and shame will be lifted. Indebtedness will be forgiven. Out of the remorse, regret, and sorrow for the needless pain and suffering humans have inflicted on cetaceans, compassion and wisdom will emerge. This will be the beginning of a new age in interspecies communication.

The immediate impact of this discovery will be a proscribing of any killing of cetaceans. The secondary impact will be the creation of a whole new field: interspecies communication. The tertiary impact will be renewed interest in other languages and other peoples within our own human species.

All this and more, with harm to none.

Alexis McKenna
Independence, Oregon

12

Bridging The Intellect And The Emotions

Fundamental knowledge is ineffable
and we mainly have access to it by intuition.

Edward Goldsmith

Several years before the dolphins came into my life, I had a memorable encounter with an archetypal figure that, while seemingly not related to dolphins, involved the sea and touched my life deeply. Eventually, I came to understand the profound implications the dream held for my interspecies work:

I am standing on a beach that looks very much like the Southern California coastline. An incredibly beautiful and powerful white mare is racing along the beach accompanied by a white colt who is her exact image, although in miniature. Like the mare, the colt has an exquisite conformation and seems the epitome of equine perfection. Over and over, the mare runs across the rocky beach to the cove, plunges into the crashing surf, swims around the point, and hauls out on the beach. The colt trails her, excited but always stopping short of entering the waves with her.

I watch the scene for a while, marveling at these majestic creatures, but particularly at the mare. Never before have I seen such a beautiful horse. But suddenly the scene takes a distressing turn. A wave catches the mare as she reenters the bay, and throws her over backward. She floats unconscious on the water's surface, limp. Terrified that she will drown, I run down to the water's edge and grab her tail. I try to pull her up onto the sand, but her mass is too great for me. I am powerless, unable to help. Suddenly, I realize that the mare somehow is me.

I shared my dream of the White Mare with an acquaintance, John Woodcock. I mentioned to John that one part of the dream left me completely baffled — the presence of the colt. John, who has a background in Jungian symbology, provided an interpretation:

This dream is a profound one, as the dreamer felt it to be. The White Mare is a theriomorphic [bestial] form of the White Goddess, usually in her destructive aspect, nightmares. If the mare is the Goddess, then the colt is her Son, and we probably have a rendering of the Mother-Son archetype. It seems that the mare is trying to draw the colt into the water and he is refusing, and, thus, is being restricted to running in a linear fashion up and down the beach. It also seems that his refusal to enter the water is connected to her distress and suffering.

The Mother-Son myth involves the necessary sacrifice of the Son for the sake of renewal. It seems that the myth is telling us that the periodic sacrifice of the masculine principle is necessary to the continuity of Life. Thus, the dream seemed to say that when the colt refuses to enter the material waters (out of fear of drowning), then all Life must suffer (the mare drowns).

Apparently, the dream is telling us that the masculine principle is refusing the sacrifice and is forced, therefore, into a linear motion, back and forth, while the Mother begins to suffer and drown. The continuity of Life is being jeopardized. The fact that the dream ended up in identity with the mare suggests that it is important for the human to feel the distress of the Mother as well as understand the problem. This dream suggests to me that each of us is being called upon to participate in the divine drama of sacrifice and rebirth of the masculine principle. By implication, our refusal to do so will have catastrophic consequences for Life.

This dream holds greater meaning for me now than before the dolphins came into my life. I have always had ecological concerns, and the dolphins are known to have the effect of heightening the environmental awareness of the people who encounter them. For me, that increased awareness seems to have taken the form of an awakening to the relationship between the symbology of the White Mare and the strong feminine, yin energy of the dolphin archetype. Simultaneously, I have gained insights into the White Mare's connection with a far more powerful archetypal figure, the White Goddess, who is the archetype for Gaia, the living Earth. In the process, I have learned to consider life in terms of the interplay between feminine and masculine forces, and to recognize that the two polarities create a dynamic conflict. In this way, the dream of the White Mare has influenced my evolving world-view.

The Latin root of science means *to know.* Science is our way of knowing, and its methods are the ways in which a culture accumulates knowledge. John Broomfield pointed out in his book *Other Ways of Knowing* that we Westerners "have made the serious error of equating our way of knowing, which we variously call science and history, with all of knowledge."[1] A diversity of approaches exists for accumulating knowledge. Indigenous science, mystical science, feminine science, and the science underlying love[2] all offer important and unique methods for gathering information, and each is relevant to our interface with the dolphins.

These ways of knowing are not the only ways that exist. Of the other ways, I an aware of one that lies within our reach — in fact, lies within us, yet, for many people, is the most difficult to access. This way is more ancient than any human system. It is the science of the animals themselves. Because this particular way of knowing lies outside of our culture, it is transparent to our human-centered schemes. I will say more about it shortly.

In each of the alternative human systems I have already mentioned, verification is vital, just as it is in Western science, although the way in which verification is achieved in another paradigm such as the indigenous world-view may seem suspect to us because of our cultural indoctrinations.[3] It can be startling in its simplicity. For example, a woman attending one of my conference presentations suggested that a verification exists for the Australian aboriginal belief in the transmigration of souls between human and dolphin forms. Having lived in Australia for a few years, she was familiar with aboriginal art, which includes a style that looks like x-ray images. An image of an animal drawn in x-ray style appears to be a cross-section of the animal, with internal organs portrayed. She suggested that x-ray art reveals the perspective possessed by a shaman who, in a previous life or shape-shifted form, has been a dolphin, since dolphins, with their sonar, are able to see internal anatomy. This story also serves as an example of how certain so-called primitive peoples, when they wanted to learn about the animal, *became the animal* — a scientific method unknown to Western science.

Robert Graves' book *The White Goddess,* which provides historical information about the White Mare and the balance between the masculine and the feminine, takes the step of becoming the animal by demonstrating how a researcher obtains information through the intuitive practice of *becoming the other,* and then goes back to the literature for confirmation. As a voice for the Goddess, Graves sacrificed his intellect and masculine principle to his emotions. In the process, he was reborn through his poetry.

Because of his experience of the White Goddess, Graves understood the masculine mind's preoccupation with logic and linearity, and its rejection of the feminine principles of intuition and strong emotional connection. Through this rejection, a limitation is revealed, as my Jungian acquaintance and dream interpreter John Woodcock explained:

> The intuitive, magical mind can handle emotion, which makes it superior to the frail logical mind. The linear mind can't pass intact through a paradigm shift; the intuitive mind can. This latter fact is precisely why the feminine mind is

gaining ascendancy now, as our culture goes through a paradigm shift that requires the sacrifice of the logical mind.

In examining the parallel histories of dolphins and humanity, we discover a curious fact. Many of the ancient peoples felt a strong connection with dolphins, as is evident in the legends of indigenous tribes and the myths that still survive concerning the prehistoric civilization of Atlantis. Later, a matriarchal dolphin-worshipping cult arose in the cradle of Western civilization, but was suppressed as the patriarchal culture of ancient Greece emerged. The ancient Greeks continued to encourage friendships with wild dolphins, though the stories from that era mention only boys.

Later, as the mantle of political power passed from ancient Greece to the Roman Empire, Western civilization began to exploit and savagely betray dolphins in public exhibitions, along with the humans and other species of exotic animals that became victims of the empire's moral decadence. Later yet in Western history, for anyone to consort with animals was dangerous for that individual. For the cetaceans, the overall consequence was that for a very long time — almost two millennia — Westerners had little to do with dolphins and whales. The biological order *Cetacea* became virtually unknown within the Western world.

Thus, a case can be made that a connection exists between the reemergence of dolphins in modern culture as a popular animal totem (a trend that has been gaining momentum since the 1960s), and the reemergence of feminine power, a movement that has escalated during the same period. Simultaneously, our scientists have created a formal discipline called *ecology,* and then taken their study of the interrelationships existing in Nature further, into *deep ecology,* which is an Earth-centered rather than a human-centered approach. All of these developments are synchronous, all are intertwined, and all are aspects of the White Goddess.

As a poet, Robert Graves knew well the power of the feminine. Because of his own personal growth process, he had become intolerant of masculine pretensions to wholeness and to not needing the feminine. Graves recognized that when the masculine sacrifices itself to the feminine, renewal is achieved; and that when the feminine sacrifices itself to the masculine, obliteration follows. These are important messages because, according to Graves, the longer the White Goddess's hour is postponed, "the more exhausted by man's irreligious improvidence the natural resources of the soil and sea become . . . [and the less merciful the Goddess will be in her vengeance]."[4] Each of us, regardless of gender, is being called to seek renewal in the Goddess, which will empower us to correct the ecological and cultural wrongs that our species is performing in the world. This admonition is consistent with the message that many people are receiving from the dolphins.

In our culture, the poets are the scientists of the emotions. They help us to view the world differently. Poetry affects us on a level that intellectual knowledge cannot, and yet, poetry is intimately connected with science. The biologist E. O. Wilson has remarked on the close parallel that exists between science and poetry, both of which "draw from the same subconscious wellsprings and depend upon similar primal stories and images."[5] It is in the context of poetry and the emotions that I now introduce into the broader picture of science the other way of knowing which I alluded to previously, the science of the animals.

In an interspecies world-view, the whales would be acknowledged as the poets of the planet. By virtue of their huge brains (in the case of the blue whale, the largest in the known universe), they might even deserve to be accorded the status of the supreme scientists of the emotions. If we listen as they sing their epic poems in the depths, they create a bridge for us to our emotions. Most people who have listened to them would say that their songs are powerful. On one occasion, when I paused 20 feet down during a surface dive to listen intently to the humpbacks' songs, I was so mesmerized by those haunting sounds that I became almost oblivious to my need to return to the surface to breathe. In the presence of the great whales, it is easy to forget connections with the land.

Roger Payne, who has studied the singing of the humpback whales for much of his life, has said,

---

> To me the most striking affinity between the musical traditions of humans and humpbacks is the impact whale songs have on human emotions. Many people are moved to tears when they hear them — as though something unaccountably ancient was overmastering them. . . . if [singing] is as ancient as I believe, it would perhaps explain why it is that we find so much meaning and emotion in music and yet cannot explain why it makes us feel the way it does. Such an impenetrable vagueness about such a basic part of our lives seems to be a sign of something whose roots lie closer to our ancient lizard brain than to our recent reasoning cortex — something with a more ancient origin than human language, which is, after all, the quintessential invention of that most recent and most prominent human trait, the cerebral cortex.[6]

Payne's point is that laws of composition, laws of ordering, and laws of symmetry all seem to exist within us at a subliminal level. These laws are probably older than our species, and may even be as old as the universe. They represent a level of knowing that we cannot access intellectually.

Some have suggested that the whales may hold certain keys for our planet, as the Earth's imponderable Source-Mind (novelist Ken Grimwood's suggestion), explorers of the domain of Being who dwell in cosmic consciousness (physician/mystic Richard Moss), and the true sovereign intelligence of this planet (Roger Payne).

Yet, however much we may admire the great whales, their minds can be nothing more to us than a remote presence with a mental life that lies beyond the comprehension of our comparatively frail human minds. At an interspecies level, our human minds may, in comparison with the minds of the great whales, be like the frail masculine mind that serves as the counterbalance to the emotional, intuitive feminine mind.

The whales' small kin, the dolphins, are the creatures we can hope to get to know and understand. Practically speaking, the dolphins are the transitional subgroup in the broad spectrum of the cetacean family. In contrast to whales, dolphins are relatively accessible to humans, and we identify with them easily. Our resonance with dolphins is probably greatly enhanced by the similarities between our brain and the dolphin brain (see Chapter 3), including the dolphins' greater connectivity between their left and right hemispheres.

But unlike dolphins, who use 50 percent of their brain even when they are asleep and at least 80 percent when they are awake, we humans rarely use more than 5-8 percent of our brain when we are awake.

These similarities and differences in structure and function suggest that we could view the dolphins as our inspiration for using our brains more efficiently and to greater capacity. Viewed metaphorically, the dolphin brain reminds us to not favor our own left-brain activities, which are analytical, mathematical, intellectual, and decisive (traditionally considered masculine traits) over right-brain functions, which represent our poetic, dreamy, and reflective nature (so-called feminine traits).

In *Dolphins*, Tim Cahill described the aftermath of an encounter with dolphins during an expedition with field researcher Kathleen Dudzinski, and identified the two broad categories into which the people who are attracted to the dolphins seem to belong:

Later you and most of the other participants are chattering away in the language of pure exhilaration. You're all talking about the morning's interaction, and what you each did, and what the dolphins did, and how it all felt. Everyone is jazzed. All most can say are things like "awesome," "fantastic," "unbelievable." Others talk about how they felt — not what the dolphins did but how the dolphins made them feel, and how it was to be in the water with them, and to feel their presence. There are others like you who feel the need to do more, to observe more closely. It's probably the difference between a scientific and a spiritual mindset. One group believes that if there is a message being communicated between human and dolphins — if that sort of interspecies communication actually exists — then it is the feeling and emotion imparted that are the important things. Not very scientific, but, well, perhaps valid nonetheless.[7]

The two categories of dolphin swimmers identified by Cahill — the scientific and the spiritual — represent the masculine and the feminine aspects that coexist within each of us, the rational and the emotional components of our humanness. If we can successfully integrate the two approaches (left brain and right brain, cognitively based and emotionally based) we will live more creatively and with greater flexibility, as the dolphins themselves do. In the process, not only will we transform our individual lives, we will help shift society toward a world-view that is ecologically sound — an interspecies world-view.

Epilogue

The companion introduced in the opening pages — my friend who wanted to swim out through the surf to the dolphins — eventually became an expert in marine mammals and found employment with the National Oceanic and Atmospheric Administration, which oversees the National Marine Fisheries Service. He fulfilled his desire to swim with dolphins as a biologist, during field research assignments in Hawaii. Today, his photographs of marine mammal species appear in federal brochures produced to educate the public about the natural history of endangered species and appropriate ways to interact with them.

It was probably someone much like my friend with whom I spoke when I called one of the National Marine Fisheries Service's regional enforcement offices to discuss the proposed changes in regulations regarding swimming with wild dolphins. That conversation went like this:

Ryan DeMares: Hello. I am calling to introduce myself as one of the people who takes groups swimming with wild dolphins.

ENFORCEMENT OFFICER: Then we should send you the federal publications that outline laws and guidelines for interacting with marine mammals.

RD: Thank you, but I already have those publications, and I am thoroughly familiar with their contents. I also am well aware of the Marine Mammal Protection Act and your agency's most recent recommendations to update it, as well as the proposed regulations that were posted on Jan. 30, 2002. One reason I am calling you today is to point out that the National Marine Fisheries Service's published bibliographies do not include my research in peak experience triggered by encounters with dolphins, which is available in the scientific literature. Of course, I realize that you were searching only the biological databases when you compiled those lists. I encourage you to extend your fact-finding activities to the social sciences and psychological records, since biological considerations give just one perspective on the matter. Also, I would like to propose that you include me, or another researcher like me, in your advisory group, to represent the human science considerations of interactions with wild dolphins.

EO: I am involved only in the enforcement end of the matter. You should discuss this with our Maryland office. I can say that we currently have a permit issued to a researcher to come in close proximity to humpback whales for photo-identification purposes. That person works with seven or eight volunteers who are rotated on a regular basis.

RD: That research sounds interesting, but again, it is biologically based. I am concerned that advancements in knowledge regarding the transformational effects of wild dolphins will be hindered if swimming with wild dolphins becomes prohibited.

EO: The establishment's attitude may be different in 50 years.

RD: In 50 years neither you nor I will be around, and the dolphins may not be either, if Low Frequency Active Sonar is deployed. But I know you are going to say that sonar surveillance of the seas is a different issue than the alleged harassment of dolphins by swimmers.

EO: Yes, and the military is not going to change.

Although in the nonaquatic periods of my life I live in the high country, I and my colleague Chris Peknic (who has the good sense to live on the coast) continue to focus on helping people to reconnect with dolphin consciousness through presentations, swim-with-wild-dolphin encounter seminars, and breathwork. We comply with the changing federal guidelines and regulations, offering, where necessary, dolphin watches and snorkeling trips instead of swimming encounters. I have always told those who join me for swims that they do not have to be in the water to have a transformational experience. As the stories in these pages have demonstrated, seeing dolphins from the boat or even dreaming about them can be a life-changing event.

As I introduce people to dolphins and the world of the sea, I continue to learn about the psycho-spiritual and transformational aspects of the human-dolphin connection, and in other ways pursue my commitment to promoting an interspecies perspective. As my studies of human-dolphin interactions have evolved, so, too, has my definition of peak experience. At one time, I defined peak as a highly significant event that involved the elated emotions; today, I think of peak experience as any event that ultimately changes the individual's world-view.

With Chris, the emphasis is on exploring the relationship between breathing and dolphin consciousness in swim-with seminars. His long-term goal is to catalyze a convergence of thought between the fields of marine biology and transpersonal psychology.

An Invitation

If you are interested in experiencing the dolphins, I invite you to consider joining The Dolphin Institute for a swim or dolphin watch and snorkeling, combined with a seminar. You can learn more about The Dolphin Institute, the subject of interspecies communication, dolphin advocacy, and our seminar schedule by visiting:

www.dolphininstitute.org,
or by contacting us at (720) 771-9963,
or by e-mail at delphinus@cybermesa.com.

ADDENDUM: REFLECTIONS ON THE CONNECTION BETWEEN DOLPHIN AND HUMAN

Chris Peknic, the founder and executive director of The Dolphin Institute, views the human-dolphin connection from the unique perspective of someone who is both a marine biologist and a therapist. He was considering the coevolution of two very different species, both highly advanced in different ways, when he wrote the following essays.

THE EQUALITY OF HUMAN AND DOLPHIN

Their lives are as fluid and peaceful as the water they flow in. We, on the other hand, can sometimes be a little too rigid and perhaps a bit harsh — the result, perhaps, of having to work against gravity all the time?

Dolphins possess attributes we humans value — freedom, vitality, grace, playfulness, serenity, trust, and love. War is unknown to dolphins, and, with rare exceptions, they do not kill each other even though they possess the capability of doing so. Like some humans, they even are known to give up their own life to save the life of another.

The question then arises, have dolphins learned something that humans as yet have not? Speaking in evolutionary terms, dolphins do have an advantage over humans since they have been around much longer than we have. Living on land most of the time, we tend to forget that this is a water planet, and that our bodies consist mostly of water. Perhaps we may be able to learn from dolphins and, in so doing, give back to them and our planet. But in order to accomplish this, we will need to broaden our human-centered view of the world.

Humans seem to have a natural tendency to cling to the familiar — a particular incident, certain emotions, relationships — even though to do so may no longer be serving us well. When we are holding on, we are not growing, we are resisting change. Then, we cannot grow. Although we survive, we stagnate.

The philosopher Tao Te Ching said, "By letting go it all gets done. The world is won by those who let it go. But when you try and try, the world is then beyond the winning."

Dolphins have an inherent quality of letting go. You can see it in their dance-like movements. When we humans dance, is it not a wonderful "letting go" experience? In much the same way, one can see "letting go" in the dolphins' fluid relationships. They move from one pod or group of friends to another, learning and then moving on. Then, they return to a previous pod. It is all done with ultimate freedom. If one could somehow perceive a dolphin's emotions, it would most likely be a similar experiencing of one emotion and then letting it go, experiencing of another emotion and letting it go, and so on. They seem to experience each emotion fully but not become the victim of it. This is truly living in the present moment. Such a consciousness is not about living in the past or worrying about the future. It is the present that is the cutting edge upon which we live our lives.

The feminine, spiritual nature of dolphins also is part of their intriguing draw, and this aspect may set a context for how dolphins base their relationships. It may also explain why women generally are more drawn to dolphins than are men. As in humans, the mother-child relationship is the primary core relationship of the dolphin. However, the other females of the pod also have a major role in the rearing of the dolphin young. The mother cares for the infant dolphin during the first two years of its life. During this time, she must also care for herself. When a dolphin mother goes off to nourish herself, the other females of the pod, the "aunties," care for the dolphin infant. An African proverb states, "It takes a whole village to raise a child." So this is another simple pearl of wisdom that these aquatic beings hold for us.

Our growing affinity for dolphins may be a sign that we are rediscovering our reverence for Nature. Can it be coincidence that people suffering from serious illnesses ranging from depression to AIDS have reported dramatic changes in their emotional state after they have been with dolphins? In some way, the dolphins assist them in releasing feelings, in experiencing happiness, and in living in the present, if only for a moment. But this moment can have a significant effect. Although encounters with dolphins may help people achieve greater serenity, they can also elicit strong emotional reactions. In addition to feeling joy, some people burst into tears when they come into close contact with dolphins. For reasons we are only beginning to explore, dolphins are capable of triggering the release of pent-up emotions or feelings that lie deep within us, even when the dolphin is on video tape or audio cassette.

Today, many people swim with dolphins and come away from the experience profoundly moved or changed. Some people experience their encounter as some type of healing experience that is difficult to put into words. We are now on the cusp of this exciting area of study, and we will see this mystery unfold in the years to come.

EXPLORING THE BREATH

When we emerge from the womb, we must take that first large gasp in order to initiate our journey. And, at the end of our life, it may be the last labored breath that ends our journey. In between these two crucial moments, we are rarely conscious of our breathing. I believe some connection exists between how we breathe and how the dolphins breathe. We can learn to breathe more effectively if we learn how the dolphins breathe. But there also seems to be something more. If we become more aware of our breath and their breath in some way, I believe we can create a closer connection between the two species.

In exploring the breath, it is important to remember that we live on a water planet. Water is made of oxygen and hydrogen, and oxygen gives us air that, in turn, allows us to breathe. The dolphins, like us, are air breathers.

To learn how this came to be, we need to go back in time. As life began to evolve on this planet, the seas formed slowly. The first anaerobic organisms gave way to aerobic organisms, which depend on oxygen for respiration.

About 65 million years ago, a catastrophic event caused the dinosaurs to die out. At the same time, the ancestors of the modern-day dolphins began to migrate from the land into the sea. Dolphins have retained air-breathing lungs, but, in the evolutionary process, flippers and tails have replaced their legs. As their forms became streamlined, their nostrils migrated from the front of the face to become a blowhole on top of the head instead of a nose. A dolphin's blowhole is naturally in a closed position and must be opened by muscular action. A muscular plug opens and closes these crescent-shaped slits, allowing the dolphin to keep water out of its lungs when it dives.

With training, we can learn to hold our breath for two or three minutes. Depending on the species, dolphins can hold their breath from seven to 60 minutes. They also have several other characteristics that relate to their unique breathing capabilities:

- In contrast to humans, dolphins must always remain consciously aware of their breath. If a dolphin cannot reach the water's surface to breathe, it will drown.
- Dolphins are known to dive as deep as 300 feet. Their collapsible rib cage allows them to withstand the great pressures of the deep.
- The water temperature in the ocean's depths is also very cold, so in order to conserve energy, the dolphin's heart rate and respiration slows down when the animal is swimming in the depths. As it begins to rise to the surface, heart rate and respiration begin to increase once again.
- A dolphin actually sleeps one-half brain at a time. By alternating hemispheres, it can allow each side to sleep while continuously maintaining its breathing pattern.
- Dolphins breathe rapidly at the surface, exchanging 90 percent of their air. By comparison, humans exchange only 5-15 percent in a breath. This rapid exchange

> charges the cetacean's blood with oxygen — a key point, I believe, for future research.

One interesting comparison between humans and dolphins is that while dolphins have retained a strong connection with air, we humans have retained a strong connection to the water. We develop in the womb in a water environment for nine months. Our cells consist mostly of water. The saline composition of our tears is virtually identical to seawater. Many of us yearn to live and vacation near oceans and lakes, which calm and restore us. The planet we call home is 70 percent water. Without water, we only survive for a few days. Nevertheless, we overlook our close connection to water and focus on the land.

Water is a more efficient medium for sound than air is, and so the dolphins and whales became sound-oriented rather than visually oriented as we humans are. But one thing did not change. Throughout their evolution, dolphins have remained dependent on air in the same form in which their predecessors consumed it on the land, and in which we also continue to consume it.

The water, whether the warm waters of the tropical oceans or the strong, cool waters of the higher latitudes, is the cradle of dolphin consciousness. The way to encounter the dolphins is by entering the water. There, in the strength and power of the sea, is the place to explore the dolphin mind. When we enter the water, the sea reawakens us to the integral connection that exists between mind and body. Temporarily separated from technology and reduced to floating minds encased in physical bodies, we enter a modality where time, weight, and self are experienced holistically. In such moments, we may remember that we and the dolphins live on this water planet together, and that both we and the dolphins share Earth's air in our breaths.

The dolphin species that exist today have been swimming in the seas for 10-15 million years now. By comparison, *Homo sapiens* has occupied the lands of the planet for about 50 thousand years. That means the dolphin varieties we know today have been on the planet considerably longer than we humans have. So, in comparison with us, the dolphins are the patriarchs on the planet. Yet, we take a human-centered view of the world, based on our conviction that we are the most intelligent creatures on Earth.

It is true that evolution has given humans a great advantage over the other creatures. Dolphins cannot physically manipulate their environment with tools. We have an opposable thumb with which to manipulate our environment. Originally, we used that thumb to create primitive tools. In a relatively short time, we used our prehensile hand to create weapons of mass destruction and to create a silicon-based life form, computers, which greatly extend our intellectual powers. Dolphin evolution has produced other special qualities. I suspect that dolphins possess a superior, expanded consciousness as the result of the way they breathe. We are beginning to realize that the analytical and manipulative skills by which we have gained a dominant position on our planet have limitations.

We need to develop other mental faculties so that we will be more balanced as intelligent beings. Could there be possibilities already long known to the creatures that are sometimes called the "humans of the seas" that we humans of the land could begin to access by learning to use our breath more effectively? I believe the answer to that question is "yes," and that as we learn more about the ways dolphins breathe we will learn new things about ourselves and our individual and species potentialities.

Dolphins appear to be involved in a constant process of being in the moment and letting go. This mode of being could be tied to their breath, possibly because, in the process of exhaling more efficiently, they are able to let go of their emotions more easily. This supposition is not as far-fetched as it may at first sound. Notice what happens when you become tense or anxious. Your first reaction probably is to hold your breath, when instead of halting your breathing you probably would benefit from breathing into your emotions by increasing your breathing.

In traditional native American cultures, animal totems are used in healing rituals, and each animal represents a particular quality. The dolphin symbolizes manna (the life force). According to indigenous teachings, the dolphin is the keeper of the sacred breath of life, and serves the people as a healing totem that helps them release emotional tension.

To understand how humans and dolphins might be brought closer together by our own conscious decision to explore the possibilities of more effective breathing, we must open up to the possibility of moving away from our current, human-centered viewpoint.

As a species, humankind can be arrogant. We believe that we are the superior species, and that harming other species is acceptable. We have been culturally indoctrinated to believe that we deserve to dominate other creatures. Although dolphins have existed in their current form much longer than humans have, we assume we are the smarter species, and we define intelligence in a way that favors our species. To step back from this perspective is not an easy task, but still, we must attempt to learn to experience the world more objectively. We can take inspiration from the dolphins, and find in them a model for utilizing our brains more holistically so that we can achieve a synergy between our left brain functions (especially, logical, rational, "scientific" thought) and our right brain functions (especially, creative thought).

Stanislav Grof, one of the pioneers of transpersonal psychology, has developed a breathing technique known as Holotropic Breathwork. Grof coined the word holotropic, which literally means *oriented toward wholeness* or *moving in the direction of wholeness.* Holotropic Breathwork involves breathing a little deeper and faster than usual, in conjunction with evocative music. Though simple, this process is powerful. By utilizing the breath more efficiently, we become capable of increasing and expanding our consciousness. This expanded state of consciousness is considered a holotropic, ultraordinary state that opens us up to other, expanded perspectives. The spiritual master Chogyam Trungpa has written of the realms of super-sound, super-smell, and super-feeling that exist beyond ordinary perception. When we are in an ultraordinary state, we become capable of experiencing archetypes, mystical states, and an expanded perception of Nature, animals, and plants as the boundaries of everyday consciousness dissolve and our psyche gets in closer touch with the creative principle. We begin to experience the present moment instead of living in the past or the future. This process helps us to drop our emotional armor and begin to connect increasingly with the universal consciousness, that aspect of the cosmos that Trungpa calls as the "cosmic mirror."

Through my work with the breath, I have discovered the potential of holotropics to facilitate our recognition that our human-centered perspective is devastating the dolphin and whale populations of the planet through a variety of activities. In tuna net and purse seine net fishing alone, an estimated seven million dolphins have died in the past 30 years. This does not include the deaths of the many other species that also become trapped in the nets. Such shortsighted practices need to be curtailed immediately and replaced with more humane methods of fishing.

Much suffering is taking place in the waters of our planet. To become aware of that suffering and take actions to stop it is the compassionate thing to do. We must learn about that which we are destroying, so that we will become less cavalier about our destructive activities.

Breathwork can help us increase our ability to connect with the dolphins, both in the water and in daily life, and to learn about them. Each of us can start right now to move toward dolphin consciousness, by taking a deep breath.

Endnotes

The Call of the Dolphins

1. Abraham Maslow, quoted in "The Plateau Experience and the Post-Mortem Life: Abraham H. Maslow's Unfinished Theory," by Tom Cleary and Sam Shapiro, *The Journal of Transpersonal Psychology,* 1995, vol. 27, no. 1, pp. 1–23.

Other Sources:

Peter Russell, *The Global Brain Awakens,* Palo Alto, Calif.: Global Brain, Inc., 1995.

Chapter 1: The Transformational Dolphin

Introductory Quote

Loren Eiseley, *The Unexpected Universe,* New York: Harcourt Brace, 1979.

1. Barbara Brunnick, personal communication, 1997.
2. Transpersonal experience is said to occur when the sense of one's identity extends beyond self to encompass more far-reaching components of Creation: the psyche, humankind, all life, or, in the case of cosmic consciousness, the cosmos. (Also see Roger Walsh and Frances Vaughan, "On Transpersonal Definitions," *Journal of Transpersonal Psychology,* vol. 25, no. 2, 1993.)
3. John Van Eenwyk, *Archetypes & Strange Attractors: The Chaotic World of Symbols,* Toronto, Canada: Inner City Books, 1997, pp. 71 & 72.
4. References regarding dolphins' fearlessness abound in the scientific literature of dolphins. Dolphin expert Kenneth Norris stated, "Porpoises are remarkably unafraid of people and that is singularly ingratiating to humans who are so used to every other wild animal fleeing at their approach" (*Marine Technology Society Journal,* November–December 1969, vol. 3, no. 6, p. 73).
5. Thirty-two species of small-toothed cetaceans, most of whom are classified within the family *Delphinidae,* are correctly called dolphins. The dolphins' conical teeth contrast with the spade-shaped teeth of the porpoise. Porpoises have three fused vertebrae at the neck, which is not a characteristic found among the dolphins. The porpoise has a blunt snout, while the dolphin's snout (scientifically called the *rostrum*) is long and beaklike (*Oceans Magazine* article by Pieter Folkens, March 1981, p. 29).

6. HeartLink information came from an online report by cranial sacral therapist Marysol Gonzalez Sterling, whose studies are online at www.biosonic.org and also at http://members.aol.com/photonica/coherence.htm. Simeon Nartoomid, a HeartMath practitioner, has confirmed to me that both vitality and peacefulness are important elements in the achievement of a state of coherence, and that Sterling's comments about HeartLink are verified by HeartMath principles and the Institute of HeartMath's human physiology research. An in-depth discussion of the coherency principle is online at www.HeartMath.org. When applied in the field, biofeedback techniques such as HeartLink offer methods for documenting the physiological effects of dolphins, and ultimately may help prove dolphins' effectiveness as healers. Information about HeartLink is available online at the Heart Harmonics Biofeedback Project Web site, www.soulinvitation.com/heartlink. Building upon her work with the HeartLink, which was created by Dan Winter, Marysol Gonzalez Sterling is now studying coherence and voice analysis. She has created a voice analysis program, *Biosonica,* that she uses in conjunction with the HeartLink, and is researching voice changes based on measurements taken before and after swimming with dolphins.
7. Cranial sacral therapy is a modality suitable for patients who suffer from cerebral palsy, autism, brain and spinal cord injury, cancer, post-traumatic stress, stroke, and other medical problems associated with pain and dysfunction. It is a gentle, hands-on method of evaluating and enhancing the function of the craniosacral system. Cranial sacral work appears to enhance the body's natural healing processes.
8. Paul Shepard, *The Others: How the Animals Make Us Human,* Washington, D.C.: Island Press, 1996, p. 94.

9 & 10. Gary Snyder, "Regarding Wave," reprinted in Bob Steuding, *Gary Snyder,* Boston, Mass.: Twayne Publishers, 1976, p. 139.

OTHER SOURCES

Denise Herzing, *Dolphins in the Wild: An Eight-Year Field Study on Dolphin Communication and Interspecies Interaction,* Cincinnati, Ohio: The Union Institute & University, 1993 (Doctoral Dissertation). Reference is made to p. 159.

Madelyn Freeman, in *The Dolphin Experience* by Lisa Tenzin-Dolma, New York: Foulsham, 1992.

Candace Pert, *Molecules of Emotion: Why You Feel the Way You Feel,* New York: Schribner, 1997.

Trisha Lamb Feuerstein, personal communication, January 2002.

Allen Schoen, *Love, Miracles, and Animal Healing,* New York: Simon & Schuster, 1995.

Abraham Maslow, *The Farther Reaches of Human Nature,* New York: Viking Press, 1971; *Religions, Values, and Peak-Experiences,* New York: Viking Penguin, 1970; *Toward a Psychology of Being,* New York: Van Nostrand Reinhold, 1968/1962.

Chapter 2: The Language Puzzle

Introductory Quotes

Kathleen Dudzinski, quoted in *Dolphins* by Tim Cahill, Washington, D.C.: National Geographic, 2000, p. 2.

Nim Chimpski, quoted in *Oceans Magazine,* March 1981, p. 4.

1. Thomas Huxley, quoted in *Next of Kin* by Roger Fouts, New York: Avon Books, 1997, p. 69. (From Huxley's *Discours de la Methode.*)

2. Nicholas Begich, *Towards a New Alchemy: The Millennium Science,* Anchorage, Alaska: Earthpulse Press, 1996.

3 & 4. Loren Eiseley, "The Long Loneliness," in *The Star Thrower,* New York: Times Books, 1978, pp. 38 and 44, respectively.

Other Sources

John Ford, "Blackfish Sound," Ontario, Canada: Holborne Distributing Co., 1992 (audio cassette).

Con Slobodchikoff. A personal communication in February 2002 updated my original information to include Slobodchikoff's work with the oval. An essay, "The Language of Prairie Dogs," appeared in *Kinship with the Animals* by Michael Tobias and Kate Solisti-Mattelon, Hillsboro, Ore.: Beyond Words Publishing, 1998.

Information about Dwight Batteau. From Gregory Bateson, "Observations of a Cetacean Community," in *Mind in the Waters* by Joan McIntyre, San Francisco, Calif.: Sierra Club Books, 1974, p. 162; Kenneth LeVasseur, "Dolphin Mental Abilities," (white paper, published online, 2000); Michael Hyson, "The Voice of the Dolphin: LFAS, the Whales, and the Navy" (white paper, published online).

Dwight W. Batteau and P. R. Markey, Man/Dolphin Communication Final Report, San Diego, Calif.: Naval Ocean Systems Center, 1967.

John Lilly. *The Scientist: A Metaphysical Autobiography* by John Lilly, Berkeley, Calif.: Ronin Publishing, 1997/1988; *Communication Between Man and Dolphin: The Possibilities of Talking with Other Species* by John Lilly, New York: Crown Press, 1978; and *Lilly on Dolphins: Humans of the Sea* by John Lilly, New York: Anchor Books, 1975.

Roger Fouts, *Next of Kin,* New York: Avon Books, 1997, p. 96.

Tim Cahill, *Dolphins,* Washington, D.C.: National Geographic, 2000.

Chapter 3: Some Dolphin Basics

Introductory Quote

Karl-Erik Fichtelius and Sverre Sjölander, *Man's Place: Intelligence in Whales, Dolphins and*

Humans, London: Gollancz, 1973.

1. SYNCHRONY. Alexandra Morton in CBS News, "Animals with a Clue," cbsnews.com, January 7, 2001.

2. Trisha Lamb Feuerstein, personal communications, 2000 and 2002. Feuerstein collects titles of books, CDs, tapes, and videos in all languages, and maintains the list online at www.physics.helsinki.fi/whale/literature/fic_main.html, in fiction, nonfiction, and childrens' literature categories.

3 & 4. From Denise Herzing, *Dolphins in the Wild: An Eight-Year Field Study on Dolphin Communication and Interspecies Interaction,* The Union Institute & University, 1993 (Doctoral Dissertation), pp. 96 and 98 respectively.

5. DOLPHIN HEARING. Sound consists of the waveforms produced when an object vibrates. Frequency is the speed at which the object vibrates. Vibrations are measured in Hertz, with 1 Hertz being equivalent to one vibration a second. Humans hear in the range of 20 Hertz to 20 kiloHertz. Higher vibrations are called *ultrasound* or *ultrasonic sound* because they are above the normal range of the unaided human ear. Dolphin hearing starts at about 100 Hertz and extends to 150 kiloHertz.

6. Michael Roads, "The Hornet Tree," in *Kinship with the Animals by* Michael Tobias and Kate Solisti-Mattelon (eds.), Hillsboro, Ore.: Beyond Words Publishing, 1998.

OTHER SOURCES

Joan McIntyre, *Mind in the Waters,* San Francisco, Calif.: Sierra Club Books, 1974.

Daniel McCulloch, personal communication, 2001. McCulloch's photography can be viewed at www.dolphinsynergy.com.

Temple Grandin, *Thinking in Pictures,* New York: Vintage Books, 1995.

CHAPTER 4: WHY DOLPHINS?

INTRODUCTORY QUOTE:

Horace Dobbs, *Journey into Dolphin Dreamtime,* London: Jonathan Cape, 1992.

1. Betsy Smith and Ric O'Barry, quoted in "Dr. Dolphin" by Judy Waytiuk, *New Age Journal,* July/August 1996, pp. 93 and 100.

2. Richard Paddock, "A New Mission," The *Los Angeles Times,* reprinted in the *Santa Fe New Mexican,* Oct. 8, 2000, F-1 and F-4; Dana Lewis, "[Soviet] Navy Dolphins Swim with Kids," NBC News, Jan. 20, 2001.

3. Nichola Webb, "The Effect of Swimming with Dolphins on Human Well-Being and Anxiety," *Anthrozoos,* vol. 14, no. 2, 2001, pp. 81-85. Nichola Webb's study was conducted at Perth's UnderWater World (now AQWA) and the Dolphin Discovery Centre, in Bunbury, Western Australia. Both of these facilities are adjacent to swimming beaches and at the time of the study were home to dolphins who were kept in natural enclosures on an artificial bay that has been fenced off from the open sea, which made them semi-

captive. Semi-captive dolphins have a more natural environment than is available in a captive containment. In theory, a semi-captive dolphin can come and go from its sea pen at will. A statement regarding the status of the dolphins used in a study — wild, semi-captive, or captive — is significant for research purposes because the natural, "unforced" behavior of wild dolphins may evoke a different response from the swimmer.

4. Nichola Webb developed separate ratings for psychological and physiological well-being before and after swims. Psychological well-being was defined as how "positive" the participants felt emotionally, and physiological well-being was described as how biologically "energetic" they felt.

5. Entrainment is the process by which dolphins promote alpha brainwave activities in humans. The dolphin entrains the human, presumably influencing the human to move into new dynamics that, to some extent, mirror the mental state of the dolphin. The model for the process is described on Simeon Nartoomid's Web site (www.unityinlove.org), which includes information about HeartMath theory and workshops. Also see www.HeartMath.org, the Institute of HeartMath's Web site.

6. Studies conducted by the AquaThought Foundation have revealed that a human subject's dominate brain frequency drops significantly after interaction with a dolphin, creating hemispheric synchronization. A baseline measurement of dominate beta (a normal state for people who are awake) was present in 92 percent of AquaThought's human subjects prior to exposure to dolphins. Post-interaction data revealed a dominate alpha brainwave pattern (associated with creativity and a state of calm) in 81 percent of the study subjects. Hemispheric synchronization (normally an uncommon condition), a positive state that promotes emotional balance, was detectable in 75 percent of the study subjects.

7. DOLPHIN INTENTIONALITY IN THERAPY. Steve Birch, *Dolphin-Human Interaction Effects*, Melbourne, Australia: Monash University/Caulfield, 1997 (Doctoral Dissertation).

8. Gregory Bateson, "Observations of a Cetacean Community," in *Mind in the Waters* by Joan McIntyre, San Francisco, Calif: Sierra Club Books, 1974, p. 160.

9. Anthony Rose, in *Kinship with the Animals* by Michael Tobias and Kate Solisti-Mattelon, Hillsboro, Ore.: Beyond Words Publishing, 1998, p. 31.

10. H. Hediger. *Studies of the Psychology and Behaviour of Captive Animals in Zoos and Circuses*, London, 1955.

11. Gregory Bateson, "Observations of a Cetacean Community," in *Mind in the Waters* by Joan McIntyre, San Francisco, Calif.: Sierra Club Books, 1974, p. 160.

OTHER SOURCES

Nichola Webb, personal communications, 2000 and 2002.

Simeon Nartoomid, personal communication, 2002.

Olivia DeBergerac, *The Dolphin Within*, New South Wales: Simon & Schuster Australia, 1998.

Mother Hildegard George, personal communications, 1997 and 2002.

Julia Vormbrock and John Grossberg, "Cardiovascular Effects of Human-Pet Dog Interactions," *Journal of Behavioral Medicine,* vol. 11, no. 5, 1988, pp. 509-17.

A. Edney, "Companion animals and human health," The Veterinary Record, April 4, 1992, pp. 285-7.

J. Voelker, "Puppy Love Can Be Therapeutic, Too," *Journal of the American Medical Association,* Dec. 27, 1995, vol. 274, no. 24, pp. 1897-9.

Ken Wilber, *The Spectrum of Consciousness,* Wheaton, Ill.: Quest Books, 1993/1977.

Michael Harner, *The Way of the Shaman,* San Francisco, Calif.: Harper, 1990/1980.

Chapter 5: Entering into Dolphin Consciousness

Introductory Quotes

After Dan Furst's Universal Festival Calendar, published on the World Wide Web and circulated on the Internet via e-mail.

Lilly's Law, from *Programming and Metaprogramming in the Human Biocomputer* by John Lilly, New York: Julian Press, 1967, p. xvi.

1. Marc Ian Barasch, personal communication, October 2001. Barasch also discussed the waking dream in his book *Healing Dreams: Exploring the Dreams That Can Transform Your Life* (New York: Riverhead Books, 2000, pp. 310-12), including its role as a step toward the spiritual realization that everything we experience is a dream.
2. A paradigm is a constellation of beliefs, values, and techniques shared by the members of a specific culture or subculture.
3. Michael Fox, *One Earth, One Mind,* New York: Coward, McCann & Geoghegan, 1980, pp. 28 and 174-5.

Other Sources

Stanislav Grof is one of the founders of the transpersonal psychology movement. See *Psychology of the Future: Lessons from Modern Consciousness Research* by Stanislav Grof, SUNY New York Series in Transpersonal and Humanistic Psychology, State University of New York, 2000.

THE NEXT STEP IN HUMAN EVOLUTION. Michael Fox, *The Boundless Circle: Caring for Creatures and Creation,* Wheaton, Ill.: Quest Books, 1996; Barbara Marx Hubbard, *Conscious Evolution,* Novato, Calif.: New World Library, 1998; Peter Russell, *The Global Brain Awakens,* Palo Alto, Calif.: Global Brain, Inc., 1995; Richard Moss, "Opening to the Infinite," Boulder, Colo.: Sounds True, 1997 (audio cassette); Jürgen Kremer, "Evolving into What, and for Whose Purposes?" in *ReVision: A Journal of Consciousness and Transformation,* Winter 1996, vol. 18, no. 3, p. 27; Pierre Teilhard de Chardin, quoted in *The Global Brain Awakens,* p. 149.

Chapter 6: Homo delphinus, Human-Dolphin

Introductory Quote

Francisco Ferraras, after setting the new world free-diving record by descending to 531 feet off the island of Cozumel. Quoted in *Outside Magazine,* April 2000, p. 32.

1. Alessandra Stanley, "A Birth Method Stirs a Debate," *The New York Times,* June 8, 1995, Section C, 8:3.
2. Bruce Mace, personal communication, October 2001.
3. Olivia DeBergerac, *The Dolphin Within,* New South Wales: Simon & Schuster Australia, 199, p. 188.
4. Joseph Bruchac, storyteller and writer of the Abenaki Nation (Vermont), quoted in *Story Earth: Native Voices on the Environment,* published by Inter Press Service, Third World News Agency, 1993.

5 & 6. Gregory Bateson, "Observations of a Cetacean Community," in *Mind in the Waters* by Joan McIntyre, San Francisco, Calif.: Sierra Club Books, 1974, p. 163.

Other Sources

Erik Sidenbladh, *Water Babies,* New York: St. Martin's Press (out of print). Igor Charkovsky's water-birthing work is also featured in "Water Baby," a documentary video produced by Karil Daniels (www.waterbirthinfo.com).

John Float, personal communication, January 2001, John Float's Web site, www.dolphinessence.com, includes information about dolphin-assisted birth preparation, dolphin healing seminars, and morning boat swims on the Kona Coast of the Big Island, Hawaii.

Information about Peter Shenstone. Drunvalo Melchizedek, *The Ancient Secret of the Flower of Life,* vol. 1, Flagstaff, Ariz.: Light Technology Publishing, 1998; Bruce Mace, personal communication, 2001.

Information about the Sirius star system. Drunvalo Melchizedek, *The Ancient Secret of the Flower of Life,* vol. 1, Flagstaff, Ariz.: Light Technology Publishing, 1998; *The Sirius Mystery* by Robert K.G. Temple, Rochester, Vt.: Destiny Books, 1987/1976.

Chapter 7: To Swim or Not to Swim?

Introductory Quotes

Plutarch, quoted in *Lilly on Dolphins: Humans of the Sea.* Garden City, N.Y.: Anchor Books, 1975.

Excerpt from U.S. Department of Commerce press release NOAA98-R105, Jan. 20. 1998.

1. Louis Herman, excerpted from "The Language of Animal Language Research," *The Psychological Record,* 1988, vol. 38, p. 349.

2. Federal Register, Jan. 30, 2002, vol. 67, no. 20, Proposed Rules, pp. 4370-82.

3 & 4. Roger Payne, *Among Whales,* New York: Dell Publishing, 1995, pp. 217 and 221, respectively.

5. From Federal Register Online via GPO Access (wais.access.gpo.gov), 50 CFR Part 216.

OTHER SOURCES

Patricia Weyer, personal communications, 2000 and 2002.

William Broad, "Evidence Puts Dolphins in New Light, As Killers," *The New York Times,* July 6, 1999, final edition, F-1.

Marine Mammal Protection Act, The Marine Mammal Commission, Bethesda, Md., 1972.

CHAPTER 8: THE SURROGATE DOLPHIN

INTRODUCTORY QUOTE

David Cole, "Emergent Technologies from Human-Dolphin Interaction Research," The AquaThought Foundation, undated white paper, p. 7.

1. Judy Bryan, "Dolphin-Safe Entertainment," *WIRED Magazine,* June 10, 1998, from www.aquathought.com's online press coverage file.

2. David Cole, "Emergent Technologies from Human-Dolphin Interaction Research," AquaThought Foundation, undated white paper, p. 6.

3. The Neurophone was invented by Patrick Flanagan, who worked closely with Dwight Batteau in the development of the dolphin language translator box (see Chapter 2). The Neurophone works by bypassing bone conduction and the hearing nerve to couple audio signals directly to nerve pathways and the brain; thus, it stimulates perception through a seventh, alternative sense. It is a powerful device for moving the brain into any desired state. Information about the Neurophone is published in *Towards a New Alchemy: The Millennium Science* by Nicholas Begich, Anchorage, Alaska: Earthpulse Press, 1996. Flanagan reported that the Human/Dolphin Communication Project isolated the encoding mechanism used by the human brain to decode speech intelligence patterns, and also decoded the mechanism used by the brain to locate sound sources in three-dimensional space. These discoveries led to the development of a three-dimensional holographic sound system that could place sounds in any location in space relative to a listener. Using this device, sound could be transmitted so that it appeared to be coming out of thin air. The project team recorded dolphins and whales in the open sea. Flanagan reported that the research team was able to accurately identify the locations of various marine mammals by using the concepts discovered in their work. The system used the same method as the human brain in locating sound sources. The reason for the Navy's keen interest in the subject is obvious and the military has explored a number of related possibilities. In

recent years, Flanagan has revealed that the experiments with dolphins and whales led to the development of large plastic ears that were tested in Vietnam. The ears were used to hear distant sounds with a high degree of accuracy, making it possible to locate the position of sounds in the jungle just as whales and dolphins had been pinpointed underwater.

4. Nichola Webb's study of the effects of swimming with wild dolphins (see Chapter 4) may help to explain this woman's experience. In Nichola's study, which surveyed people swimming in protected ocean bays without dolphins and also with dolphins, anxiety decreased after swimming with dolphins, but did not change significantly in those who swam in the same areas alone. The measurable reduction in anxiety when swimming with dolphins verifies the claim that interaction with wild dolphins reduces stress levels.
5. Tim Cahill, *Dolphins*, Washington, D.C.: *National Geographic,* 2000, p. 61.
6. Roger Payne, *Among Whales,* New York: Dell Publishing, 1995, p. 333.
7. Fred Donaldson, "On Aikido, Wolves and Other Wildlife," in *Aikido and the New Warrior,* edited by Richard Strozzi Heckler, Berkeley, Calif.: North Atlantic Books, 1985.

OTHER SOURCES

Horace Dobbs, *Journey into Dolphin Dreamtime,* London: Jonathan Cape, 1992.

Brian DuVall, New Jersey State Aquarium, personal communication, February 2002.

www.aquathought.com.

CHAPTER 9: "THE WHALES AND PORPOISES KNOW"

INTRODUCTORY QUOTE

Gary Zukav, *The Seat of the Soul,* New York: Simon & Schuster, 1989, pp. 178-79.

1. Ken Balcomb, letter to J.S. Johnson, SURTASS LFA Sonar OEIS/EIS program manager, Feb. 23, 2001.

OTHER SOURCES

Jane Goodall, *Reason for Hope: A Spiritual Journey,* New York: Warner Books, 1999, p. 162.

PCB HAZARDS. Pacific Northwest offshore waters, the home of orca pods, have extremely high levels of PCBs, and biologists consider the entire resident orca population to be at risk. PCBs accumulate in fatty tissues and are passed on to the baby orcas through the milk. Among each generation's offspring, the babies that are the first-born of each female are most severely affected because they receive the full accumulation of the toxins that have been building up for years in the mothers' tissues. For more information about this little-known but serious problem, see Ken Balcomb's Web site, www.whaleresearch.com.

CHAPTER 10: THE QUESTION OF PERSONHOOD

INTRODUCTORY QUOTES

Bernard Rollin, *Animal Rights and Human Morality,* New York: Prometheus Books, 1981, p. 82.

Carol Howard, *Dolphin Chronicles,* New York: Bantam Books, 1996, p. 290.

1. Roger Fouts, personal communication, March 2002.
2. Daniel McCulloch, personal communication, July 2000.
3. Christopher Stone, *Should Trees Have Standing? Toward Legal Rights for Natural Objects,* Los Altos, Calif.: William Kaufmann, 1974/1972, p. 53.

OTHER SOURCES

INFORMATION ABOUT SIDNEY HOLT. From *Follow the Wild Dolphins* by Horace Dobbs, New York: St. Martin's Press, 1982.

INFORMATION ABOUT THE UNIVERSITY OF HAWAII LAWSUIT. Mary Midgley, "Persons and Nonpersons," from *In Defense of Animals* by Peter Singer (ed.), New York: Basil Blackwell, 1985.

CHAPTER 11: VISIONING A WORLD DREAM

INTRODUCTORY QUOTE

Liza Tenzin-Dolma, *The Dolphin Experience,* New York: Foulsham, p. 118.

CHAPTER 12: BRIDGING THE INTELLECT AND THE EMOTIONS

INTRODUCTORY QUOTE

Edward Goldsmith, *The Way: An Ecological World-View,* Boston, Mass.: Shambhala, 1993, p. 36.

1. John Broomfield, *Other Ways of Knowing,* Rochester, Vt.: Inner Traditions, 1997, p. 1.
2. HeartLink, which is described in Chapter 1, provides a tool for describing a science of love. There also are scholars who are developing a theoretical basis and novelists who present information on methodologies. Carson McCullers, in her novel *The Ballad of the Sad Café,* presents, through the character of a street person, a methodology for developing the capacity to love anything: "I meditated and I started very cautious. I would pick up something from the street and take it home with me. I graduated from one thing to another. . . ."
3. VERIFICATION. In traditional native cultures, various procedures are used for verification, and some of these are reemerging in practices such as traditional holistic animal tracking. When in doubt of a technique or ability, the ancient animal trackers would test the skill until it proved or disproved itself. (From Douglas Gaulke, *The*

Revival of Traditional Animal Tracking: A Sensory and Spiritual Homecoming, Prescott College, 1998, Master's Thesis). Mystical science also practices verification. Marc Ian Barasch (*Healing Dreams: Exploring the Dreams That Can Transform Your Life,* New York: Riverhead Books, 2000, p. 180) mentions recognition among highly realized Christian mystics of the need to apply discrimination and analysis to their visions and dreams. The mystics of the East took similar care. Traditions such as Tibetan Buddhism have a long and venerable tradition of knowledge that includes a system of checks and balances. Historical documentation of the Dalai Lama's life (see *In Exile from the Land of Snows* by John Avedon, New York: Vintage Books, 1986) describes the caution that was applied to discerning the readiness of the State Oracle prior to the acceptance of a prophetic proclamation. Despite the high degree of spiritual attunement that one might suppose to be associated with such an oracular calling, the rituals relied on a system of checks and controls based on certain indicators. These include trance state, changes of visage and countenance, a specific mutability in the physical characteristics of the body, certain behaviors, demonstrations of superhuman agility and strength, and supernormal characteristics.

4. Robert Graves, *The White Goddess: An Historical Grammar of Poetic Myth,* New York: The Noonday Press, 1948, p. 486.

5. E.O. Wilson, *Biophilia: The Human Bond With Other Species,* Cambridge, Mass.: Harvard University Press, 1984, p. 62.

6. Roger Payne, *Among Whales,* New York: Dell Publishing, 1995, pp. 166-7.

7. Tim Cahill, *Dolphins,* Washington, D.C.: National Geographic, 2000, pp. 65 & 69.

Other Sources

Ken Grimwood, *Into the Deep,* New York: William Morrow & Co., 1995.

Richard Moss, *The Black Butterfly: Invitation to Radical Aliveness,* Berkeley, Calif.: Celestial Arts, 1986.

Addendum

Chogyam Trungpa, *Shambhala: The Sacred Path of the Warrior,* Boston, Mass.: Shambhala, 1988.

BIBLIOGRAPHY

Avedon, John. *In Exile from the Land of Snows.* New York: Vintage Books, 1986.

Balcomb, Ken. Letter to J.S. Johnson, SURTASS LFA Sonar OEIS/EIS program manager, Feb. 23, 2001.

Barasch, Marc Ian. *Healing Dreams: Exploring the Dreams That Can Transform Your Life.* New York: Riverhead Books, 2000.

Batteau, Dwight W. and P.R. Markey. Man/Dolphin Communication Final Report, San Diego, California: Naval Ocean Systems Center, 1967.

Begich, Nicholas. *Towards a New Alchemy: The Millennium Science.* Anchorage, Alaska: Earthpulse Press, 1996.

Birch, Steve. *Dolphin-Human Interaction Effects.* Monash University, Caulfield, Melbourne, Australia, 1997 (Doctoral Dissertation).

Broad, William. "Evidence Puts Dolphins in New Light, As Killers." *The New York Times,* July 6, 1999, final edition, F-1.

Broomfield, John. *Other Ways of Knowing: Recharting Our Future With Ageless Wisdom.* Rochester, Vt.: Inner Traditions, 1997.

Bryan, Judy. "Dolphin-Safe Entertainment." *WIRED Magazine,* June 10, 1998.

Cahill, Tim. *Dolphins.* Washington, D.C.: National Geographic, 2000.

Cleary, Tom and Sam Shapiro. "The Plateau Experience and the Post-Mortem Life: Abraham H. Maslow's Unfinished Theory." *The Journal of Transpersonal Psychology,* 1995, vol. 27, no. 1, 1-23.

Cole, David. "Emergent Technologies from Human-Dolphin Interaction Research." AquaThought Foundation, undated white paper.

DeBergerac, Olivia. *The Dolphin Within.* New South Wales: Simon & Schuster Australia, 1998.

DeMares, Ryan. "Human Peak Experience Triggered by Encounters with Cetaceans." *Anthrozoos,* vol. 13, no. 2, 2000, pp. 89-103.

DeMares, Ryan. "Transpersonal Aspects of the Wild-Animal-Triggered Peak Experience." *The Journal of Transpersonal Psychology,* vol. 30, no. 2, 1998, pp. 161-77.

DeMares, Ryan. *Peak Experiences with Cetaceans: A Phenomenological Study.* The Union Institute & University, Cincinnati, Ohio, 1998 (Doctoral Dissertation).

Dobbs, Horace. *Journey into Dolphin Dreamtime.* London: Jonathan Cape, 1992.

Edney, A. "Companion Animals and Human Health." The Veterinary Record, April 4, 1992, pp. 285-7.

Eiseley, Loren. *The Star Thrower.* New York: Times Books, 1978.

Eiseley, Loren. *The Unexpected Universe.* New York: Harcourt Brace, 1979.

Erskine, Barbara and Roger Jellinek. *John Pitre: The Art and Works of a Visionary.* Honolulu: Pitre Fine Arts, 1996.

Federal Register. Proposed Rules, vol. 67, no. 20, Jan. 30, 2002.

Fichtelius, Karl-Erik and Sverre Sjölander. *Man's Place: Intelligence in Whales, Dolphins and Humans.* London: Gollancz, 1973.

Fouts, Roger. *Next of Kin.* New York: Avon Books, 1997.

Fox, Michael. *One Earth, One Mind.* New York: Coward, McCann & Geoghegan, 1980.

Fox, Michael. *The Boundless Circle: Caring for Creatures and Creation,* Wheaton, Ill.: Quest Books, 1996.

Gaulke, D. *The Revival of Traditional Animal Tracking: A Sensory and Spiritual Homecoming.* Prescott College, 1998 (Master's Thesis).

Goldsmith, Edward. *The Way: An Ecological World-View.* Boston, Mass.: Shambhala, 1993.

Goodall, Jane. *Reason for Hope: A Spiritual Journey.* New York: Warner Books, 1999.

Grandin, Temple. *Thinking in Pictures.* New York: Vintage Books, 1995.

Graves, Robert. *The White Goddess: An Historical Grammar of Poetic Myth.* New York: The Noonday Press, 1948.

Grimwood, Ken. *Into the Deep.* New York: William Morrow & Co., 1995.

Grof, Stanislav. *Psychology of the Future: Lessons from Modern Consciousness Research.* SUNY, Series in Transpersonal and Humanistic Psychology, New York: State University of New York, 2000.

Harner, Michael. *The Way of the Shaman.* San Francisco, Calif.: Harper, 1990/1980.

Heckler, Richard Strozzi (ed.). *Aikido and the New Warrior.* Berkeley, Calif.: North Atlantic Books, 1985.

Hediger, H. *Studies of the Psychology and Behaviour of Captive Animals in Zoos and Circuses.* London, 1955.

Herman, Louis. "The Language of Animal Language Research." *The Psychological Record,* 1988, vol. 38, p. 349.

Herzing, Denise. *Dolphins in the Wild: An Eight-Year Field Study on Dolphin Communication and Interspecies Interaction.* The Union Institute & University, Cincinnati, Ohio, 1993 (Doctoral Dissertation).

Howard, Carol. *Dolphin Chronicles.* New York: Bantam Books, 1996.

Hubbard, Barbara Marx. *Conscious Evolution.* New World Library, Calif.: Novato, 1998.

Inter Press Service. *Story Earth: Native Voices on the Environment.* Inter Press Service, Third World News Agency, 1993.

Kremer, Jürgen. "Evolving into What, and for Whose Purposes?" in *ReVision: A Journal of Consciousness and Transformation,* Winter 1996, vol. 18, no. 3, p. 27

Keller, Evelyn. *A Feeling for the Organism: The Life and World of Barbara McClintock.* New York: W. H. Freeman, 1983.

Lilly, John. *Programming and Metaprogramming in the Human Biocomputer.* New York: Julian Press, 1967.

Lilly, John. *Communication Between Man and Dolphin: The Possibilities of Talking with Other Species.* New York: Crown Press, 1978.

Lilly, John. *The Scientist: A Metaphysical Autobiography.* Berkeley, Calif.: Ronin Publishing, 1997/1988.

Marine Mammal Commission. *Annual Report to Congress: 2000.* Bethesda, Md.: Marine Mammal Commission, March 2001.

Marine Mammal Commission. *Marine Mammal Protection Act.* Bethesda, Md.: Marine Mammal Commission, 1972.

Maslow, Abraham. *The Farther Reaches of Human Nature.* New York: Viking Press, 1971.

Maslow, Abraham. *Religions, Values, and Peak-Experiences.* New York: Viking Penguin, 1970.

Maslow, Abraham. *Toward a Psychology of Being.* New York: Van Nostrand Reinhold, 1968/1962.

McCullers, Carson. *The Ballad of the Sad Café: The Novels and Stories of Carson McCullers.* Boston, Mass.: Houghton Mifflin, 1951.

McIntyre, Joan. *Mind in the Waters.* New York: Charles Scribner's Sons, 1974.

Melchizedek, Drunvalo. *The Ancient Secret of the Flower of Life.* Vol. 1. Flagstaff, Ariz.: Light Technology Publishing, 1998.

Moss, Richard. *The Black Butterfly: Invitation to Radical Aliveness.* Berkeley, Calif.: Celestial Arts, Berkeley, 1986.

Payne, Roger. *Among Whales.* New York: Dell Publishing, 1995.

Pert, Candace. *Molecules of Emotion: Why You Feel the Way You Feel.* New York: Schribner, 1997.

Rollin, Bernard. *Animal Rights and Human Morality.* New York: Prometheus Books, 1981.

Russell, Peter. *The Global Brain Awakens.* Palo Alto, Calif.: Global Brain, Inc., 1995.

Schoen, Allen. *Love, Miracles, and Animal Healing.* New York: Simon & Schuster, 1995.

Shepard, Paul. *The Others: How the Animals Made Us Human.* Washington, D.C.: Island Press, 1996.

Singer, Peter (ed.). *In Defense of Animals.* New York: Basil Blackwell, 1985.

Steuding, Bob. *Gary Snyder.* Boston, Mass.: Twayne Publishers, 1976.

Temple, Robert. *The Sirius Mystery.* Rochester, N.Y.: Destiny Books, 1987/1976.

Tenzin-Dolma, Lisa. *The Dolphin Experience.* New York: Foulsham, 1992.

Tobias, Michael and Kate Solisti-Mattelon. *Kinship with the Animals.* Hillsboro, Ore.: Beyond Words Publishing, 1998.

Trungpa, Chogyam. *Shambhala: The Sacred Path of the Warrior.* Boston, Mass.: Shambhala, 1988.

Van Eenwyk, John. *Archetypes & Strange Attractors: The Chaotic World of Symbols.* Toronto, Canada: Inner City Books, 1997.

Voelker, J. "Puppy Love Can Be Therapeutic, Too." *Journal of the American Medical Association,* vol. 274, no. 24, December 27, 1995, pp. 1897-99.

Vormbrock, Julia and John Grossberg. "Cardiovascular Effects of Human-Pet Dog Interactions." *Journal of Behavioral Medicine,* vol. 11, no. 5, 1988, pp. 509-17.

Walsh, Roger and Frances Vaughan. "On Transpersonal Definitions." *Journal of Transpersonal Psychology,* vol. 25, no. 2, 1993.

Walsh, Roger. *The Spirit of Shamanism.* New York: G.P. Putnam's Sons, 1990.

Webb, Nichola. "The Effect of Swimming With Dolphins on Human Well-Being and Anxiety." *Anthrozoos,* vol. 14, no. 2, 2001, pp. 81-85.

Wilber, Ken. *The Spectrum of Consciousness.* Wheaton, Ill.: Quest Books, 1993/1977.

Wilson, Edward O. *Biophilia: The Human Bond With Other Species.* Cambridge, Mass.: Harvard University Press, 1984.

Zukav, Gary. *The Seat of the Soul.* New York: Simon & Schuster, 1989.

INDEX

SEMINARS & BOOK ORDERS

- ☐ I want to join The Dolphin Institute for a seminar that incorporates a dolphin watch and snorkeling adventure or wild dolphin swim program. Please put me on your mailing list for notification about future schedules.
- ☐ I am interested in experiencing breathwork. Please put me on your mailing list for notification about your wild dolphin swim or dolphin watch and snorkeling educational programs combined with breathwork seminars.

Name ____

Address ____

City, State, Zip ____________________________________

Phone ____________________ E-mail ____________________

Return to

The Dolphin Institute

P. O. Box 1093 / Boulder, Colorado / 80306-1093

(720) 771-9963

delphinus@cybermesa.com / www.dolphininstitute.org

BOOK ORDERS:

For ordering information, please contact The Dolphin Institute Press, P.O. Box 1093, Boulder, CO 80306-1093, ph (720) 771-9963, e-mail delphinus@cybermesa.com.